KIKONGO
(KONGO)
DICTIONARY & PHRASEBOOK

T0043360

KIKONGO
(KONGO)
DICTIONARY &
PHRASEBOOK

Compiled by
Yeno Matuka &
Aquilina Mawadza

Hippocrene Books
New York

For information, address:
HIPPOCRENE BOOKS, INC.
171 Madison Avenue
New York, NY 10016
www.hippocrenebooks.com

Cataloging-in-Publication Data available from the Library of Congress.

ISBN: 978-0-7818-1410-2

Printed in the United States of America.

CONTENTS

Abbreviations

adj.	adjective
adv.	adverb
f.	feminine
gov't.	governmental
gram.	grammatical
interj.	interjection
leg.	legal
lit.	literally
m.	masculine
n.	noun
ord. num.	ordinal number
pl.	plural
prep.	preposition
sing.	singular
v.	verb

INTRODUCTION TO THE
KIKONGO LANGUAGE

A Bantu language of the Niger-Congo family, Kikongo, or Kongo (Kikôngo or Kôngo) is spoken by approximately 7 million people living in the west of the Democratic Republic of the Congo (DRC), on both banks of the lower Congo River, the southwest of the Republic of Congo, and the northwestern Angola province. It is originally from Angola, in the Mbanza-Kongo area that the fifteenth century Portuguese explorers renamed San-Salvador when they came into contact with the Kongo Kingdom. In the nineteenth century, under Belgian Congo, during the construction of the railroad Kinshasa-Matadi, a creole language called Kituba or Kikongo ya Leta (Kikongo of the State) was born from Kikongo. Kituba is spoken in cities of the lower Kongo area and the Bandundu region. It is also used to broadcast news on the national radio and television stations in the DRC. Kikongo has many mutually intelligible dialects related to its many tribes. Examples of these dialects are Kindibu, Kintandu, Kiyombe, Kimfununga, Kizombo, Kisansala, Kiyaka, Kimbala. This dictionary is based on the Kikongo-Kisi-Ngômbe or Kimaniânga dialect.

PHONOLOGY

CONSONANTS		ENGLISH EQUIVALENTS
b [b]	as in	boat
d [d]	as in	double
f [f]	as in	fun
g [g]	as in	gain
k [k]	as in	kitten
l [l]	as in	lap
m [m]	as in	mango
n [n]	as in	not
p [p]	as in	pecker
s [s]	as in	soap
t [t]	as in	taco
v [v]	as in	vain
w [w]	as in	wine
y [y/j]	as in	young
z [z]	as in	zero
mb [mb]	as in	Columbus
nd [nd]	as in	dandelion
ng [ŋg]	as in	England
nk [ŋk]	as in	incarnate
ns [ns]	as in	unsettling
nt [nt]	as in	antelope
ny [nj]	as in	Niamey
nz [nz]	as in	enzyme

Note: European speakers, who could not pronounce the nasal clustering or coalescing with the consonant stops and fricatives, also referred to as nasalized consonants, produced words without the initial n or m. Thus, for example, you have "*suka*" for "*nsuka*" (end), "*tûtu*" for "*ntûtu*" (bottle), "*tangu*" for "*ntângu*" (time/sun), "*kânda*" for "*n'kânda*" (book/letter), and "*puku*" for "*mpuku*" (rat).

VOWELS		ENGLISH EQUIVALENTS
i	as in	c<u>i</u>ty
e	as in	m<u>a</u>ny
a	as in	<u>a</u>nnual
o	as in	ph<u>o</u>to
u	as in	p<u>u</u>t

Notes:

- **Semi-vowels w** and **y** are used in combination with other vowels: [u] before [a] = [w] in "*muana*" written "*mwana*" (child); [i] before [a] = [y] in "*niama*" written "*nyama*" (animal) or [i] before [o] = [y] as in "*nioka*" written "*nyoka*" (snake), "*ngiena*" = "*ngyena*."

- Kikongo uses three tones grammatically: **high** as in "*díbu*" (straw), "*nkáka*" (pangolin); **low** as in *dìbú* (wooden bell), "*devá*" (borrow); and **high-low,** which corresponds to doubling or elongating the vowel that has the primary tone on the first and the secondary tone on the second: "*múùntu*" = "*mûntu*" (person), "*ntônta*" (temptation), "*nêna*" (defecate). However, in practice, they are not used in ordinary typography; early typewriters did not have them and readers of Kikôngo were or are knowledgeable enough to sound the appropriate words according to the contextual meaning. This dictionary uses the high-low tone whenever possible to demonstrate the semantic role it carries.

- Contraction is a very noticeable phenomenon in spoken Kikongo phrases. The apostrophe will mark the contraction's deletion. It can be carried on vowel, semi-vowel, or even consonant: e.g., *mûntu wa mbote* = *mûnt'wa mbote* (a good person); *nkânga ya mbi* = *nkâng'a mbi* (a bad way of tying); *mwana wa ami* = *mwan'ami* (my child); *nkáka ya yani* = *nkák'ani* (his/her grandfather/grandmother); *ye ba êno* = *ye bêno* = *y'eno* = *yeno* ("and you"or "with you"; "ye" is translated as both "and" and "with." However, most writers of Kikongo do not pay attention to this orthographic specification. It is only heard when they are reading a text where they are found.

- The apostrophe can also be used to mark semantic differences between words. It consists of holding the consonant, which is usually nasal, before exploding the next consonant, e.g., *nkâka* (grandfather/grandmother) vs. *n'kâka* (a tropical, long-beaked large bird); *mpâta* (way of uprooting grass) vs. *m'pâta*" (five franks); *nkôngo* (earth beans) vs. *n'kôngo* (a person of the Kongo ethnic group).

GRAMMAR

VERBS

Syntactically, Kikongo verbs may be:

1. Intransitive: *ziôka* (run); *lêka* (sleep)

2. Transitive:
    Monotransitive:
    <u>Kâng</u>a maza. (<u>Stop</u> the water.)
    <u>Di</u>a dimpa. (<u>Eat</u> bread.)

    Ditransitive:
    U<u>m</u>vana/U<u>mp</u>ana maza. (G<u>ive</u> **me** water.)
    *Dîka **mwana** dimpa.* (Feed the **child** bread.)

3. Intransitive verbs can be **locative:**
    ***Vwendi** va kiti.* (He/she <u>has sat</u> on the chair.)
    ***Tinini** ku mbazi.* (He/She fled outside.)
    ***Fukamene** mu nzo.* (He is kneeling in the house.)
    ***Zembika** mu baka.* (Hang on the wall.)

    Or **motion/directional verbs:**
    ***Wênda** ku nzo.* (<u>Go</u> home.)
    ***Wiza** eva.* (<u>Come</u> here.)"
    ***Kota** mu nzo.* (<u>Enter</u> the house.)
    ***Zioka** kuna.* (<u>Run</u> there.)

The verb "to be" "*kala*" is used as a **linking** verb:
    Bêla ke<u>na</u> bêla. (He/She **is about to be** sick.)
    Bêla ke<u>ti</u> bêla. (He/She **is** sick.)
    Ngy<u>ena</u> wa mbote. (I am good. = I am in good health.)

Or as **locative:**
    Kopo eva dy<u>ena</u>. (The cup <u>is</u> here.)

4. Sentence construction in Kikongo takes the following syntactic structure:

SVi (Subject + intransitive Verb):

Wêle. "He/She left." from *kwenda* (to go)

Katukidi. "He/She left." from *katuka* (to leave)

SVO (Subject + transitive Verb + direct Object):

Dîdi ngombe. "He/She has eaten beef." from *dia* (to eat) (**Someone/He/She** is underlying.)

Sonekene n'kânda. "He/She wrote a/the letter." from *sonika* (to write) (**Someone/He/She** is underlying.)

Mbweni mambu. "I have seen the problems." *M* is the subject of *mweni*, present perfect of *mona* (to see); [m] of "mona" becomes [b] in this tense form.

SVOO (Subject + Verb + indirect Object + direct Object):

*U**m**veni mbizi.* "He/She has given **me** meat." from *vana* (to give)

In'dikidi loso. "I have fed <u>him</u> rice." from *dika* (to feed)

SVC (Subject + Verb + Complement):

Wa mbote <u>kena</u>. "He/She <u>is</u> beautiful/good."

<u>Weka</u> wa mpembe. "He/She has <u>turned</u> white."

Kitukidi diabulu. "He/She has turned monstrous/ devilish."

5. Verb Conjugation

Verb conjugation considers adverbs of time to determine the suitable suffix that conveys the tense (T). For example, using *zênga* (to cut) we can observe the tense forms from the past (1-5) through the present (6) to the near future (7) and the distant future (8):

(1) Past 5: *Yá zênganga ntama.* "I cut the tall grass a long time ago. " (Could be three days ago or the day before yesterday, if today is Tuesday; or a long time ago.)

(2) Past 4: *Yá zênga nianga zuzi.* "I cut the tall grass on Sunday." (Two days ago, if today is Tuesday)

(3) Past 3: *Yá zêngele nianga zono.* "I cut the tall grass yesterday." (Say one day ago if today is Tuesday)

(4) Past 2: *Nzêngelenge nianga mpimpa//wunu mu nsiuka.* "I cut the tall grass last night//this morning."

(5) Past 1: *Nzêngele nianga bu kwani//minuti mosi kaka yiviokele.* "I have just//very recently cut the tall grass."

(6) Present tense (habitual): *Izênganga nianga konso-lumbu.* "I usually/every day cut the tall grass."

(7) Near future: *Se izênga/s'izênga nianga ntama-ntama.* "I am about to/going to cut the tall grass soon."

(8) Distant future tense: *Se i a zênga/Sì yá zênga niânga/siazênga mbazi//konso lumbu.* "I will cut the tall grass tomorrow//any time in the future." (Note that [e i] becomes [y] before a vowel. Contractions, elision, and assimilations are heavily used in Kikongo.)

Note: Compare particularly (1) and (5) to observe how the first-person pronoun changes in form from [i] to [n] before the verbal root {*zeng-*} along with the verbal suffixes collocating with the tense forms. In all the forms, the correlation with an adverb of time gives the signal needed to select the kind of initial bound pronoun [*i-*] or [*n*] and tense suffix [*-a*] (1) [*-ele*] (2) and (4), [*-anga*] (5) and [*se* i...-*a*] (6) and [*se iá...a*] (7) to express the intended temporal meaning.

Using the verb *dia* "to eat":
(1) *Wà diânga.* "You ate a long, long time ago."
(2) *Wá dià.* "You ate." (long ago/the other day/ three days ago)
(3) *Wadîdi.* "You ate." (yesterday, two days ago)
(4) *Dîdingi.* "You ate." (this morning)
(5) *Dîdi.* "You have just eaten." (very recently)
(6) *Udiânga.* "You usually eat."
(7) *S'idiá/s'yidia/sidia.* "I'm about to eat." (very shortly/in a moment)
(8) *Si wádia/swadia.* "You will eat." (someday)

Note also that the verb to <u>be</u> "*kala*" in its irregular forms can be used as auxiliary in the progressive aspects.

Taking the verb *dia* "eat" above, we can have:

(1) *Diá ya **kala** diânga.* "I was eating." (a long, long time ago)

(2) *Diá ya **kala** diá.* "I was eating." (two days ago, / a long time ago)

(3) *Diá ya **kele** dia.* "I was eating." (yesterday)

(4) *Diá **nkele** diânga.* "I was eating." (last night / this morning)

(5) *Diá **nkele** diá.* "I was/have been eating." (very recently),

(6) *Diá ng**yena** diânga.* "I have been eating." (every day)

(7) *Diá ng**yena** diá.* "I am going/about to eat." (in a few minutes/soon)

(8) *Diá si ya twa kala diá.* "I will have been busy eating."

Although it is possible to capture the morpho-phonemics of verbal tenses as they change according to the quality of vowels and consonants yielding (*-anga, -enge, -ingi,* and *-ungu*) in the verb syllables, suffice it to say the native speaker of Kikongo is intuitively savvy of when to use the suitable form. For example, *vova* "speak" (*vov**anga**; vovel**enge***); *nwa* "drink (*nw**anga**, nwin**ingi***); *leka* "sleep" (*lek**anga**, lel**enge***); *nungunua* "be pushed" (*nungunw**anga**, nungun**ungu***).

NOUNS

Noun classes:

Kikongo nouns **usually** function in pairs of singular/
plural (See Classes 1-2, 3-4, 5-6, 7-8). The rest of the
classes do not apply the rule.

Class 1

Nominal prefix: *mu* (sg.)

Example:

> *mûntu* (person/human/man)

> ***Mûn**tu **m**osi wa n'nene wizidi dia vava.*
> Man one big has come to eat here
> A big man has come to eat here.

Class 2

Nominal prefix: *ba-* (pl.)

Example:

> *bântu (*persons/humans/people/men)

> ***Bân**tu **ba**tatu ban'nene **ba**yizidi dia vava.*
> Men three big had come to eat here
> Three big men had come to eat here.

Class 3

Nominal prefix: *mo/u-* (sg.)

Examples:

> *môngo* (mountain)

> ***Môn**go **m**osi umento.*
> Mountain one has been climbed
> One mountain has been climbed.

> *mukáti* donut

> ***Mu**kati mosi udilu.*
> One donut has been eaten.

Class 4

Nominal prefix: *mi-* (pl.)

Examples:

miôngo mountains

Miôngo miole **mi**mento.
Mountains two have been climbed
Two mountains have been climbed.

mikáti donuts

Mikati miole **mi**dilu/**mi**diwulu.
Donuts two have been eaten
Two donuts have been eaten.

Class 5

Nominal prefix: *di-*

Examples:

diâki egg

Diaki **di**mosi **di**budikidi.
Egg one has been broken
One egg has been broken.

dimpa a loaf of bread

Dimpa dimosi **di**vîdi.
Loaf of bread one is baked
One loaf of bread has been baked.

dînu tooth

Dinu dimosi **di**kolokele.
Tooth one popped off
One tooth has popped off.

Class 6

Nominal prefix: *ma-*

Examples:

> *mâki* eggs
>
> **Mâki** *môle* **ma**budikidi.
> Egg two have broken
> Two eggs have broken.

> *mâmpa* loaves of bread
> **Mampa** *môle* **ma**vîdi.
> Loaves of bread two have been baked
> Two loaves of bread have been baked.

> *mêno* teeth
> **Mêno** *mole* **ma**kolokele. (Note: *áè>ê*)
> Teeth two popped off
> Two teeth popped off.

Class 7

Nominal prefix: *ki*

Examples:

> *kima* object/thing
>
> **Kima** **ki**mosi **ki**ena va(va).
> Object/thing one is here
> There is one object/thing here.

> *kinonia* ant
>
> **Ki**nonia **ki**mosi **ki**ena vava.
> Ant one is here
> There is one ant here.

Class 8

Nominal prefix: *bi-*

Examples:

bîma objects/things

Bîma bitatu biena va(va).
Object/Thing three are here
There are three objects/things here.

binónia ants

Binonia bitanu biena vava.
Ant five are here
There are five ants here.

Class 9
Nominal prefix: *m-/n-*
Examples:

n'tânga shin

Ntânga utolokele.
Shin it has broken
The shin has broken.

n'tûtu bottle

N'tûtu mosi wubudiki.
Bottle one has been broken
One bottle has been broken.

Class 9a
Examples:

máza water (in a glass/bottle)

Maza mamosi makelenge vava.
Water one/some was here
There was some water here.

Class 10

Nominal prefix: *m-/n-*

Examples:

> *(mi)n'tânga* shins
>
> *(Mi)n'tanga mitolokele..*
> *Shins they have broken*
> The shins have broken

> *(mi)n'tûtu/ntûtu* bottles
>
> *(Mi)n'tûtu miɲa mibudiki.*
> Bottle four have been broken.
> Four bottles have been broken.

Class 10a

Examples:

> *máza* water (in two glasses/bottles)
>
> *Máza môle makelenge vava.*
> Water two were here
> There were two glasses/bottles with some water
>   in here.

Class 11

Nominal prefix: *lu-*

Example:

> *ludími* tongue
>
> **Lu**dimi **lu**lwami **lu**lwele.
> My tongue has been hurt/cut.

Class 12

Nominal prefix: *tu-*

Example:

> *tudími* tongues

***Tu**dimi **tw**ôle **tu**lwele kuna.*
Tongues two have been hurt/cut there
Two tongues have been hurt/cut there.

Class 13
No sg/pl.
Examples:

mvîndu dust/dirt

***Mv**indu **i**monekene.*
Dust/dirt has been noticed
The dust/dirt has been noticed.

bumûntu humanism

***Bu**mûntu **bu**meni songama.*
Humanism has been displayed.

***bu**nkwîkizi* belief

***Bu**nkwîkizi **bw**aku **bu**kuvukisi.*
(Often: ***Lu**kwikulu **lw**aku **lu**kuvukisi.*)
Your faith has been saved you.

Class 14
No sg./pl. for liquid
Examples:

máza water

***Máza ma**tiámukini.*
Water has been spilled
The water has been spilled.

mênga blood
***Mênga ma**tengokele.*
Blood has been shed
The blood has been shed.

In classical Kikongo style and in most instances, the **noun** (with a nominal prefix) functioning as a **topic** in a sentence dictates agreement with the **verbal** prefix or bound **subject** in singular/plural or neutral number, the **adjectival** prefix, and even the **numeral** prefix.

Note, for example, in the analyzed sentence below:

Topic (noun with *mu/ba-* (1) number prefix + adj. (numeral with *mu/ ba-* (2) number prefix from topic + adj. qualifier with *mu/ba-* (3) from topic + verb with *mo/ba-* (4) number prefix from topic (subject).

| | (1) | (2) | (3) | (4) |

Singular: *Mûntu mosi (m)wa (mu)nene (m)wayizidi dia vava zono.*

(Note: The *mu-* in brackets has been lost in today's Kikongo.)

Plural:
Bantu bôle   ban'nene bayizidi dia vava zono.
Men   two   big   came to eat here yesterday.
Two big men came to eat here yesterday.
(Note: The [u] > [o] in *bôle* is an assimilation from [o] of *zôle* "two.")

Note: We may add a 15-16 *i/zi* **class** where the singular/plural *i/zi* has been latent but retrieved in subsequent parts of speech as in:

(I)nianzi (i)mosi ia monekene vava zono.
One/A fly was detected here yesterday.

(Zi)nianzi zole zamonekene vava zono.
Two flies were detected here yesterday.

KIKONGO-ENGLISH
DICTIONARY

adelesi (*n.*) address
Agusita August
akademi academy
akele (0.4 hekitale) acre (0.4 hectares)
akise axle
akiselelatele (*pedale ya lesanzi*) accelerator (*gas pedal*)
alume army
alumondi almond
ambasade embassy
ambilasi ambulance
Amedika United States
anesitetiki anesthetic
antifrizi antifreeze
antisepitiki antiseptic
apele appeal
Apila April
apilikoti apricot
arte art
asansele elevator
asipirini aspirin
aveni avenue
Avili April
avio airline, airplane, plane
azanse agency

ba-/bâwu they
bâdi ball; football (soccer)
bâdi dia kitunga basketball
baka (*v.*) catch, trap, take; get, receive / (*n.*) wall / (*adj.*) rare
baka mbôngo (*v.*) cash
baka nzengolo decide

bakala dia n'sômpi husband
bakisa understand
bala-bala street, avenue
bâle dia mâlu football (soccer)
balikoni balcony
balula mix; reverse
bambukila remember
bâmbula ntima remind
bânda dia nsi south
bânda nkomi punch
bandi izieniki tampon
bandi manetiki tape
bându bottom
bângula translate
bânki bank
bansimba twin
bantika start
bantika diâka resumé/resume
bantikila undo
bântu people
bântu bakisalu staff
bânza (*n.*) idea / (*v.*) think
bânzala kia bato deck
bânzala kia ndeke airport
bânzala kia nsaka stadium
bânzala kia nzo clear ground in front of the main house entrance
bânzila (*v.*) suspect; think for
batakana (*adj.*) close
bateli battery
bato boat, ship
batukwa lid
bat'wa bantu ferry

baya wood
bêbisa (*v.*) tire
bêla (*n.*) illness / (*v.*) be sick
bêla kwa mfulumuna asthma
bêla kwa mvuzangana ntima mu m'bu seasick
bêla kwa nzietolo motion sickness
benda drain; pull, withdraw
benda matu warn, (*lit.*) pull the ears
benda maza flush
bêndo funeral
bênduka (*v.*) move
benduzula torture
besi nsi nation
bi-/biawu they
bia of/for (*prep. for plural of **ki/bi** nominal class*)
bia kabana (*adj.*) separate (*of separate nature*)
bia ndemosolo tiya fuel (*for starting fire*)
bia nsungi seasonal
bia simi (*adj.*) chemical (*of chemical nature*)
bia zinsi zanza international, of countries of the world
biabîngi many (*of countable items*)
biamfulu bedding (*of the bed*)
biamfunu supplies (*for use*)
biamunzo domestic, for the house
biandata carry-on (*for carrying out*)
biandia bia nsuka dessert
biandwa (*n.*) drink
biansadila supplies (*for work / to work with*)
biansûnga seasoning (*for food*)
bibila bible
bibulu bia ntwela cattle
bidia food

bidiki brick
bidîngwa jewelry
biêle beer
bikinzu pottery
bila reason / **bila (nki)** why
bilo desk; office
bilo kia nkotolo front desk
bilo kia nsângu information desk
bilo kia pulisi police station
bilo-kia-posita post office
bilôngo drug, medication, medicine, remedy;
  n'kânda bilôngo prescription
bilongo biantibiotiki antibiotics
bima bia mvwânda ye lêkila furniture
bindokila bia tiya fireworks
biôle pair
bisalu bia besi nsi folk art
bisalulwa kit
bisi bus
bisikaleti bicycle
bisisulwa ruins
bitatila alcohol, liquor
bitwelezi cattle
bivânanga bêla mu nitu virus
bizinisi business
bobini (*ya nsinga sengwa*) spring (*metal coil*)
boda smoke
bôka declare; shout, yell
bôkila (*v.*) call, summon, invite
bola rot
boloko jail, prison
bolosi kia mêno toothbrush
bombe ash

bômbi bomb
bombo candy
bônga pick up
bônso (*v.*) seem; (*prep.*) like
bonso bwa sîsa bambuta traditional
bôsi then
bôti boot
buba blister
bûba nkuba torture
bubu actual; now
búdi quantity (*of something like meat*)
búdi dia mbizi steak
budika broken
bûka mênga bleed
bûku book
bûku dia ntwadisi guidebook
buku dia zinkumbu directory
bukuna cut
búla (*v.*) type; kick
búla moko clap
búla mpiololo (*v.*) whistle /blow the whistle
búla ngûnga (*v.*) ring/hit the bell
bule blue
búlu animal; hole
búlu dia maza (*n.*) well (*for water*)
bulukutu mint
búlwa be shot
bûmba hug
bumosi (*n.*) single/oneness
bumputu poverty
bumûntu humanism
bûnda thigh
bundakasa add

bûngi fog
bunkufi resumé/resume
bunsôngi justice
bunswêki privacy
bûnu today
busadilwanga normal, regular, standard
busadilwanga ntângu zambidi usual
busi sister
búta deliver (*of a baby*)
buto button
butukila native
bwa (*v.*) fall
bwabwana (*v.*) meet
bwamûntu mosi privacy
bwasîsa bambuta tradition, what ancestors legated
bwâti (*n.*) box
bwâti-ya-posita postbox
bwe(yi) how, what
bwêle kiambi pest
bwêle kianzo pet
bwêta massage
bwîvi fraud

cositime suit (*also* **kositime**)

dala sheet
dalapo flag
dati date
dati ya mbutuka date of birth
dentifilise toothpaste
Desemba December
devisa (*v.*) loan
dêzo bean

diá dine, eat
dia kabana separate (*adj.*)
dia kindûmba romantic
diá kiûvu (*v.*) ask, question
dia kondwa luve illegal
diá kwa mwini lunch
diá kwa nkokila dinner
diá kwa n'sûka breakfast
dia-kwa-paleke picnic
diá ndefi swear
dia ndwênga wise
dia ngengesi sensitive
dia ngolo serious
dia n'siku illegal
dia nwa kimfumu official
dia sekele of a secret; to be kept secret
dia ta bambuta idiom, what the ancestors said
diabeti diabetes
diâka again, also
diâki egg
dialudi true
diâmbu (mu diâmbu) in this case, issue, because
diâmbu dia mpasi problem
diâmbu dia mvîmba phrase
diambú diá nki why
dianseyila funny
dianswâlu emergency
diantântu drama
dianzaki emergency
dibânza thought
dibuta family
didi this
diena-salulwa plan

diezele diesel
dikâlu trolley
dikisionele dictionary
dila cry
dimensio size
dimpa bread
dimuka dive; drown, sink
dina that
dinkondo dia n'koyongo banana
dînu tooth
disitiliki district
disu eye
disuku local
díve wing
divé aisle
divunia cotton
diwizanono OK, okay
dokima document
dokotolo doctor
dolale dollar
doti dirt
dumuka jump
dungasa (*v.*) rock
dungasa threaten
dusi lavatory
dwani customs

edi this
ekala screen
eki this
eku here
emele e-mail
empirimante printer

emu here
ena (*v.*) is, are; (+ **V-anga**) been
endu this
enge (*interj.*) hello; hey
enzeniele engineer
esiti east
Etazini United States
eti + **V-anga** (*v.*) been
êto our
eva here
evo or
ewu this

fakisi (*n.*) fax
falamasi drugstore, pharmacy
falaze sentence (*gram.*)
Fevilie February
fiba kiss; suck
fidisa fakisi (*v.*) fax
fifûnda parcel
fihotele motel
fikopo jar
fila send; **(kwa mûntu)** transfer
fila ku-ntwala postpone
fila mu ntang'wa kunima postpone
fila nkânda mu posita (*v.*) mail
filigo refrigerator
filime film
fimpatu fia bia nkuna (*n.*) garden
finangana (*adj.*) close
fîngu insult
fintângu instant, moment
finzo fia ndêka mviokolo hostel

fiônga thin
fiôti less, little, minor, small
fioti fisidi about
fitapi rug
fiûma some
fololo flower
folomazi cheese
fôni phone
fôni mobile mobile phone
fôni ya bandônga public telephone
fôni ya bântu babo public telephone
foto photograph
foto ya mwînda flash photography
fu kia mputa scar
fu kiambote quality
fufu flour
fuka cover
fukutila allergy; flu, influenza
fulale scarf
fûlu oven
fulu area, location, place
fulu kia kati kia nsumbila shopping center
fulu kia kula plug
fulu kia masuku ma nzingila apartment
fulu kia mvûndila shelter
fulu kia ndeke airport
fulu kia ndîla lounge
fulu kia ndwîna malavu (*n.*) bar (*place for drinking*)
fulu kia nsansila bibulu farm
fulu kia nsimbisila bima depot
fulu kia nsuka destination
fulu kia nsukula ya bisi bus terminal
fulu kia nswamina refuge

fulu kia ntalululu checkpoint
fulu kia ntelamasa parking
fulu kia nzingulu address (*n.*)
fulu kia zibuka field
fulu kia zinzo za mvwanda camp
fulu kiantadila bibulu biamfînda zoo
fulu-ki-mvovila platform
fuluka full
fulumuna (*v.*) breathe
fulusa fill
fumfu purple
fûnda (*v.*) accuse / (*n.*) pack, package; thousand
fûndisa (*v.*) referee; (*leg.*) judge
fûndu stomach
fungununu bumblebee
fusakana (*adj.*) ground
futa pay, repay
futa mboko (*v.*) bribe
futila (*v.*) rent
futila spend
futisa (*v.*) toll
futisa mpaku (*v.*) tax
futubale soccer
futulu paid
futumuna recycle, revive
futwa paid
fwa die
fwâna (adv.) enough, much / (*v.*) fit
fwanana equal
fwanisa fitting
fwasakana corrupt
fwasikisa litter
fwele (*n.*) brake

fwêmisa irritate
fweti (*adj.*) mandatory / (*v.*) ought, require

galame gram
galamele grammar
gato cake

Hebeleo Jew

i (*e.g.*, **di-/ki-**) it
ibobo exact; OK / (*interj.*) well
ibobo kibeni accurate
ibubu exact
ibuna kibeni accurate, exact
îh yes
ina (*v.*) am
ine + V-anga (*v.*) been
înga yes
ingeta yes
inifolome uniform
inivelesite university
insilina insulin
insulansi insurance
Inteleneti Internet
Inteleneti ya kôndwa n'singa wireless Internet

ka bobo ko incorrect, wrong
ka bwa(u) ko no
ka bwa(wu) ko incorrect
ka kima ko nothing, zero
ka kûma ko nowhere
ka lekwa ko nothing, zero
ka nsa mosi nkutu ko never

ka ntalu ya yingi ko inexpensive
kabana share
kabini ya fôni phone booth
kabula (*v.*) separate, share
kabwawu ko wrong
kadi because
kâdila dictate
kafi coffee
kaka just, only
kakamana choke
kakawo cocoa
kala (*v.*) be (**ina** am; **ena** is, are; **kele/kedi/kezi/
   kezingi/kelenge** was, were; **ine/ena/eti** + V-anga
   been)
kala môyo be alive
kala ye m'funu (*v.*) need
kala ye nsatu want
kala ye vumu (kia mwana) pregnant
kalaka officer
kalasi class
kalasi kia n'nene university
kalasi kia ntete first-class
kalasiki classic
kalati card
kalati kia fôni phone card
kalati kia mfuka credit card
kalati kia n'toto map
kalati kia nzayil'wa muntu ID card
kalati kia nzila road map
kalati-kia-posita postcard
kalavâti (*n.*) tie
kale square (*form*)
kaloti carrot

kaludi ko false
kalunga ocean
kamio truck
kanale channel
kânda tribe
kânga (*v.*) trap, arrest; tie; close, shut; record
kânga mu kiôzi freeze
kânga mu kumba lock
kânga mu mafuta fry
kângama closed
kângama kwa kiôzi frozen
kângama kwa vumu constipated
kângama ye join
kangidila lock out
kangula unlock
kangulu kia maza faucet
kani-nkutu (*adv.*) never
kansi but
kapala plastic
kapoti condom
kapu chapter
kati middle
kati dia mpimpa midnight
kati-kati center; mild
katuka leave
katukidi left
katula drain; exclude, remove, withdraw
katula kaka except
katula nzevo shave
katula pusiele (*v.*) dust
kawusu rubber
kayengele altitude
keba beware

kebila protect
kedi (*v.*) was, were
kela (*n.*) bullet / (*v.*) gossip, criticize someone
kele (*v.*) was, were
keledi credit
keleme cream
keleme ya manzevo shaving cream
kelenge (*v.*) was, were
kênde pie
kengila (*v.*) guard
kesa soldier
kezi was, were
kezingi was, were
ki nza nkulu traditional
kia bansôla (*adj.*) restricted
kia kisi n'tôto secular
kia lukofi formal
kia lukwikilu reliable
kia luvuvamu safe
kia luzitu polite
kia mâvu formal
kia maza fluid
kia mono (*pron.*) mine
kia mûntu mosi private; private property
kia (mûntu) yandi mosi individual
kia nkatudul'we nsudi deodorant
kia nkuna transplant
kia n'siku legal
kia nsimbikisa concrete
kia nsûngi seasonal
kia ntuba disposable
kia n'zôle (*adj.*) second (*ord. num.*)
kia sumbula hazard

kiabola rotten
kiâdi sad
kiadôka flat
kiadoti dirty
kiafwa dead
kiakiozi (*adj.*) cold
kiakondwa nzayilu unconscious
kiakulan electric
Kialendi Monday
Kialumingu Sunday
kiambote hello; **kiambote kiaku** hello (*to an individual*); **kiambote kieno** hello (*to more than one person*)
kiambukuta (*n.*) snack
kiambweno mpasi uncomfortable
kiâmi (*pron.*) mine
Kiamonde Monday
kiampila n'ka special
kiampimpita complicated
kiâmvu bridge
kiandata portable
kiankayilwa gift
kiankulu antique
kiantuba trash
Kianzôle/Kian'zôle Tuesday
kiânzu spring (*season*)
kiapâti pastry
Kiasabala Saturday
kiasântu holy
Kiatânu/Kian'tânu Friday
Kiatatu/Kian'tatu Wednesday
kiavulu door
Kiaya/Kian'ya Thursday

kiâzi million
Kiazole Tuesday
kibakala sex (*of male sex/gender*)
kibeni kosher
kibuti folk
kidiasala lizard
kidie kia ndûnda vegetarian
kiêlo door
kiêse (*adj.*) pleasant, joyful / (*n.*) fun, happiness; **dia kiêse** thing of pleasantness/joy/fun / **mona kiêse** (*v.*) feel happiness, have fun
kifinuku lid
kifunda baggage, luggage
kifunga skirt
kifwâniswa picture, photograph; sample; monument
kifwâniswa kianzoka (munti evo mu tadi) sculpture
kikalaka bureaucracy
kikênto sex (*of female sex/gender*)
kiki this
kikondolo mikolobe sterile (*germ-free*)
kikotisa introduce oneself
kikûku kitchen
kikûndi relationship
kiliniki clinic
kilogrami kilogram
kilometa kilometer
kilutidi excess
kima arm; item, something, thing
kimakesa army
kimanga epileptic
kimantunu kia sikalie escalator
kimazi photograph, picture

kimbângi reference
kimbêvo illness
kimenina plant
kimenina kia n'toto organic
kimfumu authority
kimfwetete (*n.*) fly (*insect*)
kimona-mêso plain
kimongo-mongo hill
kimpa scene; theater (*hall/room*)
kimpa kia nsi scenery
kimpampa (*n.*) trick
kimpângi relationship
kimpola underwear
kimvuka (*n.*) club, league, political party, union /
   (*adv.*) together
kimvuka kia bankwa lulendo rebellion
kimvumina milk
kimvwâma fortune
kimvwe kia kinswêki private property
kimwana-mwana child, infant
kina (*adj.*) that / (*v.*) dance
kinati conductor
kindende (*n.*) minor, youth
kindende kia nkênto girl
kindezi kia mwâna childcare
kindokila kia mpangula bomb
kindûmba romance
kinganga art
kinganga kia besi nsi folk art
kingelezo English language
kingizila immigration
kîngula (*v.*) visit
kinkita trade

kinkoso knee
kinkuti shirt
kinlôngo synagogue
kinsekwa flea
kinseva-seva (*n.*) smile
kinswêki private
kintudimoya insect
kînzu pot
kiobila lavatory
kiôzi kia bêla (*n.*) cold (*illness*)
kîpi club
kipupa epileptic
kisadi activist; agent; employee; operator
kisadi kia bilo officer
kisadi kia luzolo (*n.*) volunteer
kisadi kia min'siku senator
kisadisa self-service
kisalu activity; business, job, occupation, work;
  partner
kisalu mpasi busy
kisalulwa equipment
kisântu sacred
kisâsi kia mbizi butcher
kisi kanda ethnic
kisînsu symbol
kisita sterile (*for a female*)
kisoda military
kisoda kia maza ma n'nene (*n.*) navy
kisongisa introduce oneself
kisundidi biabio most
kitalatala mirror
kiteke statue; **nkisi wa (ki)teke** epileptic
kiteke kia n'nene monument

kitêndi ribbon
kitendi kia nlele cloth
kitendi kia n'nwa napkin
kiti chair
kiti kia malulu wheelchair
kiti kia mpûnda saddle
kiti kia mvelo saddle
kitini section
kitoko (*n.*) romance / (*adj.*) romantic
kituka become
kitunga basket
kitunga kinsumbila shopping basket
kiûvu inquiry, query
kivâna (*v.*) surrender
kivovi lawyer, attorney
kivovi kia min'siku lawyer, attorney
kiyîngi beggar
kizalu flood
koba lip
kobadi cabinet
kobadi dia kumba locker
kodi ya mbokolo dialing code
kodi ya nsi country code
kodi ya posita postal code
kodidisa cure
kodidisa mpasi painkiller
kokama become pregnant
koko bull
kôko hand
kólo knot
kôlo glue
kolwa overdose
kompani company

kompani dia ndeke airline
kôndo (*n.*) type
kôndo wa menga blood type
kondomi condom
kóndwa vacant
kôndwa without
kóndwá futila free
kôndwa kiese unhappy
kóndwá kwa futa dwane duty-free
kóndwá kwa luzitu impolite
kóndwá kwa mbakulwa poverty
kóndwá kwa mbakusulu misunderstanding
kóndwá kwa nsola mandatory
kóndwá kwa nzola hostile
kôndwá luzitu rude
kôndwa mâzu evo ndingana quiet
kôndwa-ndâmbu neutral
kôngo (*n.*) score
kôngula collect
konko corner
konkutila knock
konsila consulate
konsili consul
konso any, every
konso kima anything
konso kuma anywhere
konso muntu anybody
konso muntu mosi anyone
kontabele accountant
kontala contract
konti account
kônti ya banki bank account
kopi copy

kopo cup
kosimetiki cosmetics
kota enter, join
kota mu kimvuka (*v.*) associate
kotika knife
kotisa inject
ku kukwîza ntângu future
ku landi ko ignore
ku n'dimba mbânza downtown
ku nima midi afternoon
ku nsi down
ku vile downtown
ku zulu up
kudimukilanga ntângu west
kukwiza ntangu eventually
kulan electricity
kulele ya color
kûlu leg
kumbazi (*adv.*) out
kumbaz'ya nzo (*adj.*) outdoor, outside
kûmi ten
kûmi dia m'vu decade
kûmi-ye-mosi eleven
kûmi-ye-nâna eighteen
kûmi-ye-nsambwadi seventeen
kûmi-ye-sâmbanu sixteen
kûmi-ye-tanu fifteen
kûmi-ye-tatu thirteen
kûmi-ye-vwa nineteen
kûmi-ye-ya fourteen
kûmi-ye-zôle twelve; **nanga kûmi ye zôle** dozen
kúmu beach, shore; harbor, dock
kûna there

kunima after, behind; future; **masidi kunima** that remains in the future

kûnku quantity

kunkukia n'tôto territory

kunsi below, under

kuns'ya ntoto underground

kuntwala after; **makwiza kuntwala** that will come in the future

kuntwâla future

kûse ya mvwata diaper

kusuna wipe

kus'ya (ntûla) ntu pillow

kutolo asleep

kútu ear

kutula undo

kuvaikilanga ntangu east

kwanda far, away

kwânga loaf

kwe nsukina destination

kwe(yi) where

kwêla marry

kwelele married

kwênda go

kwenda kwa nsambisi wa zulu appeal

kwênda-vutuka round-trip

kweyele ntângu later

kwîka (*v.*) ignite

kwikila believe

kwîle leather

kwîza come

kwiza nati bring

labele tag

ladio radio

lâla dia nsa lemon

lala dia n'zênzo (*n.*) orange

lamba (*v.*) cook

lânda follow

landidila late

lândila then; next

lândila va nima next to

lapi pencil

lapolo report

laputopi laptop

lasio ratio, ration

lawuka mad

lazwâle razor

lebele rebel

lebelio rebellion

lefizé refugee

lêka sleep

lekitangele rectangle

lekwa something

lembwa unhappy

lembwa fwâna insufficient

lembwa nwînwa fûmu non-smoking

lembwa sadilwa ntângu zazo unusual

lembwa sungama incorrect

lembwa wizana disagree

lembwa zayakana unfamiliar

lemvukila forgive

lenda able

lênda natwa portable

lenda sadilwa available

lendakane possibly

lene wool

lenge melon
lenvukila (*v.*) pardon
lepibilike republic
lesanze gasoline, petrol, gas
leta state
letula letter
levile yeast
lezevwale ya lesanze gas tank
lezime regime
libeleli bookstore
lisansi license
litele liter
lobinet faucet
lômba (*v.*) request
lômba ndoloki apologize
lômba nlevo apologize
lônga dish
longa dia n'nene basin
longa-dia-yalumuku plate
lôngo wedding
longuka learn, study
lóóngo medicine
lóóngo biankangila mabuta contraceptive
lóóngo kia nsadisila mpasi aspirin
lôsa throw
lôso rice
lubandanu thunder
lubânzi rib
lubu mosquito
lubwabwanu appointment
ludi truth
lugibi rugby
lúka vomit

lûka beware
lukâlu train
lukâlu lwa nswâlu express train
lukaya page; leaf
lukolo alcohol
lukuni wood
lûlu wheel
lumbu day
lumbu-ka-lumbu permanent
Lumbu kia Bwanana New Year's Day
lumbu kia kisalu weekday
lumbu kia lubutuku birthday
lumbu kia mbutuka date of birth
lumbu kia mvu wa mbutuka anniversary
lumbu kia nsuka expiration date
Lumbu kia ntete kia mvu/mvula New Year's Day
lumingu week
lunâna eighty
lûnda (*v.*) keep, save
lûndulu storage
lupângu fence
lupitalu hospital
lusadisu (*n.*) aid, help
lusalusu lwa buku dia zinkumbu directory
  assistance
lusambwadi seventy
luse face, front
luta prefer
luta buke less
luta m'funu (*adj.*) chief
lutâmbi (*n.*) step
lutila (*adv.*) more
lutumu commission

lutumwa order
luvê permission, permit, right
luvê lwa ntakudila fishing license
luvibudulu patience
luvunu lie
luvuvamu peace, safety, security
luvwa ninety
luwa mushroom
luwawanu constitution
luwizanu contract
luyâlu administration, government
luzayisu announcement
luzingu life
luzingu lwa mpîmpa nightlife
luzitu (*n.*) respect
luzitu lwa kimfumu royalty
luzwâlu razor
lwaka arrive
lwâla hurt
lwêka offend
lwênga avoid
lwenguka (*adj.*) spare

ma kia ndundila reservoir
ma kinswêki secret
ma kisi n'tôto secular
ma n'kululul'wa mpasi sedative
Madami Mrs. (*title*)
madia food, meal
madia ma kimvumina dairy
madia ma m'bu seafood
madia ma nswâlu fast food
madia ma ntînu fast food

mafuta fat, oil
makângu partner
makazini shop, store
makazini ma biandia grocery store
makazini ma bilongo drugstore, pharmacy
makazini ma bima bianteka convenience store
makazini ma n'nene ma bianteka department
  store
makazini ma tombola secondhand store
makinu dance
makum'masambanu sixty
makum'matanu fifty
makum'matatu thirty
makum'maya forty
makum'mole twenty
Malasi March
malavu wine
malavu mangolo liquor
malêmbe (*adj.*) slow; smooth
malukozamu convenient
maluvê ma bumuntu human rights
Mâma Mrs. (*title*)
Mama fiôti Ms. (*title*)
Mama mwâna nkêto Ms. (*title*)
mâmbu trouble
mambu ma Nzâmbi religion
mamêla nun
mamvwemvwe cheap, inexpensive
mana sumbwa sold out
manaka calendar
mandeka asleep
mandwa beverage
manisa exhaust

mansadila program
mansevila comedy
mânta climb; ride
mânta tingi-tingi (*v.*) skateboard
manteka butter
mantima engraving
mantisa mount
mantungul'we nsi infrastructure
masa ma mputu wheat
masambakanu contagious
masêla nun
masini machine
masini ma bisono printer
masini ma foto camera
masini ma ngyumisina dryer
masini mansongisila ntînu speedometer
masini mansukudila nlele washing machine
masonia ma mwana nswa baby wipes
masunia moustache
masuwa ferry, ship
maswa poison, venom
matala-tala eyeglasses
matalasi mattress
matîti grass
matôndo kwa nge(ye) thanks to you
matôndo mâku thanks are yours
matwâdi reporter
mayêla disease
Mayi May
maza liquid, water
maza ma color
maza ma lâla yellow
maza ma mbuma juice

maza ma niâza green
maza makangama kwa kiôzi ice
maza matiya gasoline
mazi fat
mâzu noise, sound
mâzu ma luzayisu siren
mâzu mangolo loud noise
mazunu fever; flu
mbabumuka surprise
m'baki mia mboko corrupt
mbakul'wa mbôngo income
mbakulwa ya mbôngo (*n.*) cash
mbala potato
mbaluka turn
mbându example
mbangala summer
m'bângudi translator
mbantukulu beginning
mbânza city, town
mbata peak (*top of*)
m'batakani neighbor
m'bati pants
mbati-mbati neighborhood
m'bat'ya nsi underwear
m'bat'ya zini jeans
mbazi tomorrow
mbêbisa (*n.*) tire
mbebolo damage
mbela near
mbela kati (*adj.*) medium
mbela mbanza suburb
mbela-mbela around, nearby
mbele knife

mbêbisa pollution
m'bend'wa matu warning
mbêni enemy
mbêvo (*n.*) patient
mbi (*adj.*) bad, wrong / (*v.*) harm
mbidi much
mbidika kettle
mbiêkolo promotion, crowning
m'bikud'ya mambote fortuneteller
mbizi meat
mbizi ya maza fish
mbiz'ya ngômbe beef
mbiz'ya ngulu pork
mboda smoking
mbokolo (*n.*) call
mbokolo ya bima mu nsi import
mbômbo nose
mbôngo money
mbôngo za mfuta fee
mbôngo za mfutila nzo (*n.*) rent
mbôngo za nsîmbisa deposit
mbôngo za nzênza foreign currency
mbôngo zidiwanga mu nsi currency
mbongu za mfuka credit
mbonika view
mbonokon'we kimbêvo diagnosis
mbonokono profile
mbonosono symptom
m'bota bâdi dia nzuba bat (*sports equipment*)
mbote (*adj.*) good nice / (*interj.*) hello; **kia mbote**
  greeting
mbote bêni beautiful; great
mbot'ya nsuka perfect

m'bu ocean, sea
mbudika concussion
m'bud'ye miziki musician
mbulwa shot
mbuma berry; pill
mbuma n'ti fruit
mbuma sangu corn
mbuma tolo sleeping pills
mbuma za nkuna seed
mbuma za nzenzo grape
mbumba cat
mbumbulutela potato
mbundakasa total
mbundakasu amount
m'bungisi fog
mbûnzu forehead
mbuta old, adult; **Mbuta** Mr. (*title*)
m'buti parent
m'buti wa bakala father
m'butu product
mbutul'wa mbôngo economy
mbutulu delivery (*of a baby*)
mbwa dog
mbwabwani meeting
mbwâki red
mbwangasa advertisement
m'bwangu wa ntu migraine
mbwêno ntima mpasi (*n.*) worry
mbwêno ya mpila nsadila system
mbwînu sight
mekaniki mechanic
même lamb, sheep
mena salua project

mena vangwa (*n.*) promise
mênga blood
meni menu
Mesie Mr. (*title*)
mesile measure
mêso zungana drowsy
metele meter
mêza table, altar
mêza ma nsonikina desk
mfiângu kidney
mfidusulu mu posita postage
Mfid'ya mpaka Protestant
m'filu fig
mfînda forest
mfînda nkobo jungle
mfisima itch
mfúka debt, loan
mfûka ruins
mfula flower
mfulu bed
mfuluka n'koko flood
mfuluka nsuka maximum
mfumu senior
mfumu ya bilambi chef
mfum'wa bilambi chef
mfum'wa kisalu employer
mfum'we luyalu president
mfum'we nsi president
mfûndi pasta
mfûndi ya kwanga dough
m'fûndisi (*n.*) referee
mfundulu accusation
m'funu purpose

mfuta (*n.*) toll
m'futidi tenant
m'futu compensation, prize
mfutulu expense, payment, repayment
m'fututu wa tiya twa zima ash
m'fut'wa kisalu mu mbôngo salary
m'fut'wa mfuka cover charge
mfwankayi rough
m'fwe matu deaf
m'fwelemi nurse
mfwenima sterile (*for a male*)
mi-/miawu they
mia n'kululul'wa mpasi sedative
midi midday, noon
mika mia même wool
mikolonde microwave
mîle mile
miletwale fireworks
mimvwatu clothing
mina (*v.*) swallow
miniti minute
(mi)n'kânda (*n.*) mail
minkawu mia mputu crutches
min'lele clothing
Misioni Protestant
mizé museum
miziki music
Mizilima Muslim
modepase password
mokina talk
mona see
mona mpasi (*adj.*) painful / (*v.*) feel pain, suffer
mona mu nitu feel

mona ntima mpasi (*v.*) worry
mona wônga be afraid, experience fear
môngo mountain
monika bonso appear
montele (*n.*) clock, watch (*timepiece*)
mosi one
mosike mosque
motele engine, motor; motel
moto motorcycle
mpa (*adj.*) fresh, new; **mwana mpa** new baby
mpaka cage; protest
mpaku (*n.*) tax
mpaku ya banzala kia ndeke airport tax
mpak'wa ntekolo sales tax
mpamba empty
mpâmbu intersection
mpâmbu a mbânza square (*town square*)
mpânga verb
mpângi folk, relative
mpangula cord
mpasi (*adj.*) difficult, serious / (*n.*) pain
mpasi mu mona rare
mpasi za mianzi arthritis
mpasi za ngânzi (*n.*) sore
mpasudulu surgery
mpasula surgery
mpasululu surgery
mpatu farm
mpavala zero
mpêmbe white
mpeni naked
mpila kind
mpila luyâlu regime

mpila mosi even, same, uniform
mpîmpa night
mpîmpa mvîmba (*adv.*) overnight
mpimpita mystery
mpiololo (*n.*) whistle
mpitakani puzzle
mpofo blind
mpotefe wallet
mpovo free
mpovolo za dwani customs declaration
mpu hat
mpuku rat
mpuku-lu-nuni bat (*animal*)
mpûnda horse
Mputu (Ns'ya mputu) European Union
Mputuki European
mpwênia proper, pure
mu kati dia nzo indoor
mu kati kwa through
mu lawu lucky
mu mawonso general
mu mvanunu servant
mu nganzi angry
mu nswâlu rapid
mu nswâlu bêni express
mu wôla hour
mudiambu dia because of
mukati (*n.*) cake / (*adv.*) inside
mulembwa sômpa (*adj.*) single
mungenge olive
mungizila immigrant
mûngwa salt
munkond'wa diambu innocent

munkôndwa m'futu (*n.*) volunteer
munkondwa nzo homeless
munsala shellfish
munsi low
mûntu mosi (*n.*) someone / (*adj.*) personal
muntudia worm
muntudimoya person
mûnt'wa bakala nkwa ntok'wa babakala homosexual
mûnt'wa bakala wakula man
mûnt'wa boloko prisoner
mûntwa ludi honest
mûnt'we mfutila tenant
munzila through
mupepe air, wind
musitikele mosquito net
muswalu wa mavimpi sanitary napkin
m'vâlu horse
mvânguka injury, disability
m'vânguki disabled
mvângula violence
mvang'ya mambi terrorist
m'vâni server
m'vâni a nsamu reporter
mvanunu appointment; service
mvanun'wa mangwele vaccination
mvayika menga ma bukento menstruation
mvayikulu exit
mvedoso toilet
m'velo bicycle
mvelula (*n.*) rape
m'vewo bonus
mviba seam

m'vîmba entire
m'vîmbu swelling
mvindumuka circle
mvinga (*n.*) change
mvinga ngolo revolution
mvingasu substitute
mviôka (va fulu kia n'siku) trespassing
mvita (*n.*) battle; riot
mvitia n'tu leader
mvololo withdrawal
mvolopo envelope
m'vond'ya bibulu hunter
m'vovo word
mvovolo accent
m'vu year
m'vu ukwîza next year
m'vu ulwêki next year
m'vu uviôkele last year
m'vu ye m'vu ever
mvukama (*n.*) assault
mvûkisa rescue
mvula (*n.*) rain, shower, storm; year
mvula maza ma mpembe (*n.*) snow
Mvula mpa New Year
mvula za nkudila age
mvûnda break, holiday, rest
mvundulu vacation
mvunguka lumbu dawn
mvutudila (*n.*) refund
mvutudulu repayment
mvutuka (*n.*) return
m'vu-ye-m'vu permanent
m'vwa fulu occupant

mvwa luzitu courtesy
Mv'wa mpa New Year
mvwalangani disaster; misunderstanding
mvwalasi suitcase
mvwamunu (*adj.*) deep / (*n.*) wealth building
m'vwatu wa ngiobidila bathing suit
m'vwât'wa fêti (*n.*) dress
m'vwât'we ndêkila pajamas
m'vwe employer, owner
mvwîlu property
mwâlu lane, path, trail
mwâna child, kid
mwâna bakala boy
mwâna kalasi student
mwâna mbuta wa n'kento daughter
mwâna ndûmba girl
mwâna nkazi wa bakala nephew
mwâna nkazi wa nkêto niece
mwâna nswa baby
mwâna wa bakala son
mwânzi nerve; vein
mwânz'ya nima spine
mwâsi naked
mwêlo exit
mwêl'wa nkotila entrance
mwesi fulu occupant
mwesi kintwâdi (*n.*) associate
Mwesi mputu European
mwesi nsi ya ngyala civilian
mwesi-nzo occupant
mwînda lamp, light, flash
mwînda tolose flashlight
mwîsa wônga scare

mwîvi robber, thief
mwîv'ya makazini shoplifter

nâna eight
nani who
napî quiet
nata carry, transport
nata (n'tomobilu) drive
nata ku nsia n'kaka export
navigasio navigation
ndâ long, tall
ndambá pea
ndâmbu region; side
ndambu a kati-kati half
ndâmbu mosi ya n'ya quarter
ndâmbu ya member
ndâmbu ya nzo ya sina basement
ndâmb'wa kiansadila spare part
ndâmb'wa n'ka opposite
ndâmb'wa nsi district
ndandulu suite
ndandul'wa nzila direction
ndatunu transportation
ndatunu ya babo public transportation
ndatun'wa madia mu suku room service
ndeke airplane, plane
ndekolo accommodation
ndezi (ya mwana) babysitter
ndia food
ndiamu cemetery
n'diâti pedestrian
n'die wa ndûnda vegetarian
ndikidila ya madia food poisoning

ndînga language, voice
ndînga nzênza foreign language(s)
n'dingu wa nsi midnight
ndio if
ndisu cent
ndodokolo apology
ndoloki apology
ndômbe black
ndômbolo (*n.*) demand, request
ndômbol'wa nlêmvo demand for apology
ndondokolo departure
ndônga crowd; population
ndongokolo za mâmbu seminar
ndongolo education
n'donguba tall
ndu bânzulu (*n.*) suspect
ndudi bitter
ndûmba lady
ndûmba nzolwa girlfriend
ndûnda vegetable
ndûnda leti lettuce
ndûnda salata salad
ndundila reserve
ndundulu reservation
ndundulu ya bisalu economy
ndungasa (*n.*) threat
ndûngu pepper
n'dungu barrel
ndungutila heat, warm; temperature
ndûnza kutu earache
nduta border
nduta za ntînu speed limit
ndwakulu arrival

ndwakul'we mbote welcome
ndwêlo young
ndwêlo ya nsuka minimum
ndwênga wisdom
nêla ring (*jewelry*); window
neze (*n.*) snow
nga ndio if
nga vo if
ngalamatisi arthritis
ngânga bifu psychologist
ngânga bilongo physician
ngânga m'pasudi surgeon
ngânga nkalulu psychologist
ngânga n'kisi doctor
ngânga n'sadi engineer
ngânga nzâmbi priest
ngânga ya meno dentist
ngânzi (*adj.*) sore / (*n.*) anger
nge (*interj.*) hello, hey / (*pron.*) you
ngêmbo bat (*animal*)
ngêye you
ngialumusu advertisement
ngiambila conference
ngikamu junction
ngîndu idea
ngitukulu bêni mystery
ngiumbula bee
ngo maza shark
ngolo (*adj.*) hard / (*n.*) might, power, strength
ngômb'ya bakala bull
ngônda month; moon
ngônda wîki kwa toko ye ndûmba honeymoon
Ngônda ya kumi ye mosi November

Ngônda ya kumi ye zole December
Ngônda ya m'vwa September
Ngônda ya n'kumi October
Ngônda ya n'nana August
Ngônda ya nsambanu June
Ngônda ya nsambwadi July
Ngônda ya n'tanu May
Ngônda ya ntatu March
Ngônda ya ntete January
Ngônda ya n'ya April
Ngônda ya nzole February
ngongol'wa laka throat
nguba peanuts
ngudi mother
ngud'ya nkazi uncle
ngulu pig
ngûnga bell, ring (*sound*)
ngûnga luzayisu alarm
ngûnga nzayikuswa tiya fire alarm
nguya eyeglasses
ngûya matala-tala eyeglasses
ngwawani compromise
ngwizani agreement, compromise
ngyabul'wa mbizi za maza fishing
ngyadulu ya bantu kwa bantu democracy
ngyambulu front desk
n'gyambul'wa bântu hospitality
ngyantukulu beginning
ngyêmba fraud
ngyobila bath
ngyúvu (*n.*) question
nianguna chew
niânzi (*n.*) fly (*insect*)

nianzi za n'tu lice
niâza onion
niemangasa massage
nikuka (*v.*) move
nikuna mu ngolo (*v.*) rock
nikuzuka motion sickness
nima back, rear
nîngama halt, stop; layover
ningana (*v.*) move
nioka snake
nitu body
nivo level, rate
nkadi bad
n'kaká other
n'kâka bakala grandfather
nkâka n'kênto grandmother
nkakila barrier; jam (*traffic*)
nkakila ya mavunia tampon
nkakila ya vumu kia mwana condom
n'kak'wa ntângu sunblock
nkalu jug
nkalul'wa bila reasonable
nkama hundred
nkama mvu century
n'kânda letter; **(mi)n'kânda** (*n.*) mail
n'kânda bilôngo prescription
nkânda kimbângi receipt
nkânda kimbângi kia mbutukila birth certificate
nkânda mbântina mu ndeke boarding pass
n'kânda mfuka bill
n'kânda ndînga grammar
nkânda nitu skin
nkânda nsângu newspaper

nkânda ntekolo sales receipt
nkândi nuts
nkândi ya kokoti coconut
nkânga (*n.*) tie
nkangama n'tima heart attack
nkangama vumu constipated
n'kangami prisoner
n'kangami wa kingolo hostage
n'kângu group
nkangulu (*n.*) arrest
n'kanu decision
nkati very
nkatu (*adj.*) empty / (*adv.*) no
nkatukulu departure
nkazi brother
n'kaz'ya bakala husband
n'ke small
nkela ya posita postbox
n'kele gun
n'kelo fountain
nkênda (*adj.*) sorry / (*n.*) sorrow
n'kengedi (*n.*) guard
n'kênto wife, woman
n'kênt'wa luzitu lady
n'kês'ya maza ma tiya battery
nkewa monkey
nki ma what
nkiena (*prep.*) like
nkiena kulele ya titi kia yuma brown
n'kíla tail
nkîndu (*n.*) riot; war, battle
n'kîngudi visitor
nkîngulu (*n.*) visit

n'kisi medicine
n'kiti merchant
nkodila health
nkokila evening; **(yiyi/ya bûnu)** tonight
n'kóko river; water
nkômbo goat
nkome fist
nkondolo vacancy
nkongo hunter
n'koti mu kimvuka (*n.*) associate
n'koti ya kimwîvi intruder
nkotisa import; introduction
nkotolo (*n.*) access, entry
nkufi short
nkulula discount
nkûmb'wa ngyikila surname
nkûmbu name
nkumbu mosi once
nkumbu za mbidi often, many times
nkûmbu zôle twice
n'kum'ya kintudimoya insect repellant
n'kûndi friend
n'kûnd'ya luzingu partner
nkûnd'ya mwana bakala boyfriend
nkûnga song
n'kûngi festival, party
n'kung'ya ngibila ye bisikwa concert
nkuni firewood; woods
nkununu culture
nkûnzu raw
nkutu knapsack
nkutu ya lusadisu lwa ntete first-aid kit
nkwa diabeti diabetic

nkwa kiêta disabled, handicapped
nkwa lulêndo (*n.*) rebel / (*adj.*) full of pride
nkwa menga makuluka anemic
n'kwânga (*n.*) saw
nkwikul'wa mwinda lighting
nk'ye ntângu when, what time
n'laku flame
nlâmbi a nkênto maid
nlândi companion
nlayi rail
nlele mia nsukula laundry
nlele wa ntunga fabric
nlêmbo finger
nlêmb'wa n'nêne thumb
nlêmvo (*n.*) pardon
nlômbi beggar
nlonga list
nlônga diâmbu sentence (*grammatical*)
n'lông'e nda queue
nlôngi teacher
nlongoki student
nlông'ya kalasi kia zulu professor
nlông'ya mbaz'ya kalasi tutor
nludi roof
nluta profit
n'natia nsamu messenger
n'nene big, large
n'nwá mouth
n'nwanis'ya luyâlu rebel
noka (*v.*) rain
noka mvula maza ma mpembe (*v.*) snow
nolo north
nolo-esita northeast

nolo-wesita northwest
nomba number
nomba ya fôni phone number
nomba ya mvwândulu seat number
nomba ya ntilumuka flight number
nôti note
Novemba November
nsa sour
nsa mosi once
nsabi key
nsabukulu across
n'sadi bimpa actor
n'sadisi (*n.*) aide, assistant
nsadulu (*n.*) use
nsadul'wa min'siku legislature
nsadul'wa mpatu agriculture
nsadul'wa ntângu schedule
nsâk'wa nima backpack
nsaka (*n.*) game, play, sport
nsaka za badi dia ndwanina rugby
nsakanasa entertainment
nsâku bag
nsâku ya ndekila sleeping bag
nsâku ya nima backpack
nsalulu (*n.*) act
nsalul'wa bambuta tradition
nsalul'wa mbôngo expense
nsálul'wa ntima pulse
n'sâmba footpath, path, alley
n'sâmbanu sixth
nsambidila chapel; **nzw'e nsambidila** house of
  prayer
n'sambisi judge

nsambwadia seven
n'sâmpa shelter
n'sâmpa kapo tent
nsampatu shoes
n'samu case (in this ~); event; message
n'sânga necklace
nsângu information, news
nsansulu education
n'sâs'ya mbizi butcher
n'satu hunger, starvation, famine
n'sat'wa luka nausea
nsat'wa ngolo (*n.*) need, shortage, lack of
nsat'we maza thirst
nsekodol'wa mâmbu interpretation
n'sekod'ya mâmbu interpreter
nsezemo flare, lightning
nsi bottom; country
nsiensolo ya mbôngo currency exchange
nsiens'ya kûma weather
nsikidis'wa nkodila health insurance
n'siku rule, law
nsikwa shot
n'sik'wa ngemono mu mpîmpa curfew
nsimbulu touch
n'singa cord, rope, cable
n'singa mia nsambudila tiya jumper cables
n'singa sêngwa wire
nsîngu neck
nsîng'wa kôko wrist
nsoba (*n.*) change
nsobol'wa kûma climate
nsoko liver
nsôla selection

n'solo goods
nsôlolo election, vote, option
n'soma fork
nsombukila flea
nsômpa (*n.*) loan
nsompani marriage
nsônga nziêtolo va nsi navigation
nsôngi sharp
nsongisa example
nsôngolo (*n.*) show
nsongosolo (*n.*) exhibit
n'soniki author; journalist
nsonokono registration
nsosolo (*n.*) search
nsosolo a ngângu ye ndwênga science
nsudi odor, smell
nsuka (*n.*) end, last, limit
nsûka dawn, morning
nsuk'a benga cliff
nsuka lumingu weekend
nsuka n'dia nene appendicitis
nsuka ntangu deadline
nsuki hair
n'sukudi wa masini ma ngyumisina dry cleaner
n'sûmbi client, customer
nsûnga (*adj.*) delicious / (*n.*) flavor
nsûngama (*n.*) right
nsûngi period, season (*of a year*)
nsungikilu order
nsung'ya nsotuka makaya autumn
n'suni muscle
nsusu chicken
nsûtuka surprise

n'swâlu (*adj.*) fast, quick / (*v.*) hurry / (*n.*) speed; **ndut'e nswâlu** speed limit; **kisongi kia ndut'e nswâlu** speedometer

n'swâmi refugee

nswengina asthma

n'sweswe baby

nswikidi sugar

nsya luyâlu state

ns'ya ntoto basement

n'ta sour

ntakamu (*n.*) assault, attack

n'takudi fisherman

ntakula fishing

ntalu price, cost, calculation; math

ntalu mpasi expensive

ntalu ya nsobolo exchange rate

ntalulu ya mvayikulu check out

ntalululu (*n.*) check

ntal'wa fioti cheap

ntal'wa ngolo expensive

ntal'wa suku room rate

ntama-ntama soon

ntambakani infection

n'tâmbu (*n.*) trap

n'tambudi pedestrian

n'tambudid'ya mambi guilty

ntambudul'wa bântu hospitality

ntambukusu communication

ntâmbula (*n.*) walk

ntambululu admission

n'tâmbusi (*n.*) guide, conductor

n'tanda flea

ntangumuka immigration

n'tangumuki immigrant
ntand'wa nsi north
ntang'wa mwini daytime
ntang'wa nkufi temporary
ntâng'wa tômbe night
n'tâng'ya mbôngo accountant
ntângu (*n.*) second (*in time*); time; sun
ntângu va mbata n'tu midday, noon
ntângu yi lembolo manu ever
ntangu zazo always
ntatikwa kutu earache
ntawuzi student
nteke mud
n'tékólo grandchild
ntékolo sale
n'tekwa nima against
n'tek'ya makazini shopkeeper
ntel'wa mambu conference
ntelamasa (*n.*) arrest; standing; **fulu kia ntela-masa ntongobilu** parking
ntentemb'wa maza octopus
ntete first, before
ntêtuka concussion
ntezakasa measure
ntêzolo trial
n'ti ye n'singa ntakudila fishing rod
ntilumuka flight
n'tima heart
ntînu (*adj.*) fast, quick / (*n.*) speed
n'tin'wa nkênto queen
nto spring (*water*)
ntombe dawn
n'tomis'ya zidi barber

ntomo flavor, taste
ntomobilu automobile
ntondele thank you (I thank you)
ntongobilu vehicle
n'toto earth, ground, land
n'toto wa zinzo zamvwanda campground
n'tot'wa nzo floor
n'tôt'we simenta pavement
n'tu head
ntulu cough
ntululu ya biansûnga seasoning
ntululu ya mupepe wa mbote air conditioning
ntûmbu needle, syringe
ntûmbulu prosecution
ntumunu commission
ntumwa messenger
ntumwa kinzonzi diplomat
ntumwa luyalu ambassador
ntumwa luyalu lwa nzênza consul
ntûnga mu nit'wa n'káka transplant
ntûngulu institution, settlement, building;
  architecture
n'tûtu bottle
n'twâdi a n'samu reporter
n'twâla front
n'twênia fresh, young
nukilele nuclear
numolo number
numolo ya fôni phone number
nûnga win
nunu old
nviôka vumu diarrhea
nwa (*v.*) drink

n'wa hole
n'yabi wa mbizi za maza fisherman
nzâ world, nature, universe
nzadi river
n'zâka jacket
nzakama n'toto earthquake
nzáki (*adj.*) fast, quick, hurried; fluent / (*v.*) **tanga nzáki** read fluently / (*n.*) **dia nzáki** emergency; **suku dia nzáki** emergency room
nzaku border
nzalu spoon
n'zânza nkatu desert
nzayil'wa kisalu professionalism
nzayil'wa muntu identification
nzayilu experience
n'zayisi announcer
n'zengo decision
n'zêng'ya nsuki barber
nzênza (*n.*) stranger, foreigner, unfamiliar person; guest
nzênzo sweet
n'ziêti passenger; tourist
nzietokolo detour
nzietolo trip
nzietolo mu bifulu sightseeing
nzila itinerary, route
nzila bisêngwa railroad
nzila lukongolo ramp
nzila mâlu footpath
nzila nkwênda mosi one-way
nzila n'layi railroad
nzila n'nene road
nzila nsya n'toto subway; tunnel

nzila ns'ye ntoto metro station
nzila ntomobilo highway
nzitukulu (*n.*) charge; tying of the knot
nzit'wa nkênto mother-in-law
nzo house
nzo kia stadium
nzo ndundila mabuku library
nzo ya fûlu kia mampa bakery
nzo ya mfundusulu court
nzo ya n'kanda mia nteka bookstore
nzo ya nzâmbi sanctuary
n'zod'ya matoko ye bandumba heterosexual
nzola (*n.*) love
nzola dia appetite
n'zonza argument
nzônzi spokesperson
nzônzi ya min'siku attorney, lawyer
nzûnga turn
nzûngana meso dizziness
n'zung'wa ntu dizzy
nzûngu pan
nz'wa kafi café
nz'wa kimpa theater (*hall/room*)
nz'wa kinzonzi parliament
nz'wa mvundila inn
nz'wa mvwânda home
nz'wa ndêka ya mviokolo hotel
nz'wa ndîla restaurant
nz'wa ndundila mbôngo bank
nz'wa n'nene ya sambu cathedral
nz'wa nsukudila nlele laundromat
nz'wa ntomosono repair shop
nz'wa ntumwa luyalu lwa nzênza embassy

nz'wa nzâmbi church, sanctuary
nz'wa nzâmbi ya mizilima mosque
nz'wa sâmbu sanctuary
nz'wa zându dia n'nene supermarket

okisizeni oxygen
Okutoba October
olidinatele computer
opela opera
otomatiki automatic
otoni autumn

paki pack
palapidi umbrella
palato tray
paleke (*v.*) park
pandu (*n.*) pound
papela paper
papela ya aluminumu aluminum foil
papela ya nkusunina n'nwá napkin
papie ya nkokunina toilet paper
pasepolo passport
pasipalomi grass
pâti pasta
paze page
pedale pedal
pedale ya nsiensila ntînu clutch pedal
pelemi ya ndatun'wa ntomobilu driver's license
pelezida president
pêlo mirror
pete-pete soft
pêza weigh
piano piano

pilamidi pyramid
pine ya dôka flat tire
pinta pint
pitiloya petrol, kerosine
pitsi peach
pizama pajamas
pola lose
polele lost
politiki politics
pologalami program
polotefe purse
polovinse province
pomi apple
pompa (*v.*) pump
pompi (*n.*) pump
posi pocket
potopoto jam; cream; mud
pubilisite advertisement
pulisi police
pulu-pulu diarrhea
pulusa percent
pusa push
pwazo poison
pwe point
pweme poem

reyo ikis x-ray

sabuni soap
sabuni dia maza detergent
sadila (*v.*) use; (~ **mbôngo**) spend
sadisa (*v.*) aid, assist, treat
saka hunt

sakana (*v.*) play
sakisa zealous
sakodo backpack
sâla stay
sála (*v.*) act, make, work, do
sála kimpampa (*v.*) trick
sála kôndwa m'futu (*v.*) volunteer
sála mu nzola (*v.*) volunteer
sála/sá mazu (*v.*) cry, make noise
salulwa tool
salulwa kia miziki musical instrument
sâmbana declare; scream from pain
sâmbanu six; **n'sâmbanu** sixth
sâmbila pray
sâmbu dia n'ka opposite
sâmbula bless
sam'pani champagne
sandale sandals
sandwisi sandwich
sânga island
sangabudi spider
santele center
santime cent
sanu comb
sanzema ya ntînu gear
sâsila explain
sasuka available
sateliti satellite
se father
sekele secret
sekeletele secretary
sekisio section
sekula pour

sekula mambu interpret
seleyale cereal
sena senate
senatele senator
sêngwa iron, metal
sêngwa kia mbôngo silver
sêngwa kia nzimbu coin
sentile ya kiti seat belt
Sepitemba September
seva laugh
seva kinseyila (*v.*) smile
siampu shampoo
sianse science
SIDA AIDS
siêlo (*n.*) bar (*place for drinking*)
sieni chain
siên'ya nkângila (kinkuti evo m'bati) zipper
sika (*v.*) shoot
sika mpiololo (*v.*) whistle, blow a whistle
sika nsiala clap
sikaleti cigarette
sikalie stairs
sikama awake, wake
sikanele scanner
siki (*v.*) ski
sikidika confirm
sikila ready
sikulu school
sikulwa kia miziki musical instrument
sikwa shot
sima cement
simitele cemetery
simu beach, shore

simu dia bankwa mpeni nudist beach
sina base
sinamo cinnamon
sindima camera; cinema, movie
siniatile signature
sinsu sign, signal
sinzidi (*n.*) guard
siôka narrow, thin
sisa deliver (*of goods*)
sisitemi system
sitade stadium
sitandale standard
sitasio station
sitasio ya lukalu train station
sitwaye citizen
sivu winter
sizo scissors
soba alter, change, exchange
soda soldier
sofele conductor
soka (*v.*) load
sokisa influence
sokola chocolate
sôla (*v.*) select
solula find
somba ball
sombala football, soccer; spell
somisi shirt
sônga (*v.*) show
sônga vângu (*v.*) tip
sôngila mfunu qualify
sôngisa (*v.*) exhibit, show, display
sonika write

sonokono kia tinta pen
sosa (*v.*) search, seek
sosaze sausage
soseti sock
sosi sauce
soya soy
stasio ya metolo metro station
su pipe (*for tobacco*)
sudi south
sukadi sugar
sukisa (*v.*) limit
suku room
suku dia kinswêki private room
suku dia lusadisu lwa nswâlu emergency room
suku dia mvingila changing room
suku dia ndeka bedroom
suku dia ndikuzun'wa nitu gym
suku dia ndîla dining room
suku dia ngiambidila conference room
suku dia ngiobidila bathroom
suku dia ngyambidila lobby; salon
suku dia n'nene suite
suku dia n'nene dia nzo hall
suku dia ntezolo fitting room
suku dia nzáki emergency room
suku dia sambu chapel
suku dia tadi cave
sukula wash
sûmba buy, purchase
sumbula accident; danger, risk
sume towel
sume ya ngiobidila bath towel
sumu dia luyalu crime

sunda biabio (*adj.*) main
sunda zola prefer
sundidi extra
sundila (*adv.*) more
sungama (*adj.*) correct
sûngama *(v.)* go straight, be straight / (*adj.*)
  straight, right / **nzila ya sûngama** the straight
  road
supu soup
swâmunu refuge
swasikisa compare, distinguish, discern
swaswana different
swêka conceal, hide
swêka mu ns'ya n'toto bury
swênga narrow
swenwa choke

tâ tell
tá say
tá mansaya swim
tadi (*n.*) rock, stone, lime
takama (*v.*) assault, attack
takisi cab, taxi
takula (*v.*) catch, fish (*from water or a hole*)
takula kuvanunu luve fishing permitted
tala look
talafiki traffic
talasimisio ya otomatiki automatic transmission
talulula (*v.*) check, review, take a second look
tambakane infected
tambakasa transfer
tâmbi foot
tambudila accept, admit, recognize

tambukisa infect, transfer

tâmbula (*v.*) step, walk; receive

tânga read

tantala complain, lament

tânu five

tapi carpet

tata father; sir

Tâta Mr. (*title*)

tata mbuta uncle (*older paternal*)

tatika bite

tatikul'wa kia ma kiamôya insect bite

tatikwa dînu have a toothache

tatu three

teatele ya sindima movie theater

teka sell

tekolo sold

têla (*v.*) dictate / (*n.*) drop (of liquid)

telama stand, stop

telamasa (*v.*) arrest, stop; **telamasa munt'wa mbi** stop the bad guy

telefoni telephone

telemasa (*v.*) park; **telemasa ntongobilu** park the automobile

televezio television

temba stamp

tempelo synagogue, temple

tênda kia nkangila mputa bandage

tesite test

têza try

tezikisa estimate

têzo measure

ti (*n.*) tea / (*prep.*) until

tiâba rip

tiamuna pour
tiki fare, ticket
tiki kia bato boarding pass
tiki kia kwênda-vutuka round-trip ticket
tilibinale court
tilumuka (*v.*) fly
tilwale drawer
tima dig (*with an instrument*)
tîna avoid
tîndika push
tingi-tingi (*n.*) skateboard
tini piece
tini kia nsi region
tini kia ns'ya luyâlu province
tînta ink
tîti herb
tiya fire; **ngolo za tiya** energy
tiya twa ngyoka hot
tiyo pipe (*for water*)
tobula puncture
tokanasa irritate, harass, annoy
toluka broken
toma kula flourish
toma tala examine, inspect
tombe dark
tombula lift
tomisa repair, improve, beautify
tôta collect, pick up
tû- we
tuba throw, hurl, toss
tûdila vûvu (*v.*) trust
tûku source
tukuta sweat

tûla (*v.*) load, put in
tûla kôngo (*v.*) score
tûla maza ma kulele dye
tûla mu bwâte (*v.*) box
tûla n'siku prohibit
tûla tiya ignite
tûla va zulu mount
tumântu tomato
tûmba prosecute, punish
tûmbu penalty, sanction
tûnga knit; sew, stitch; build
tunganana (*v.*) watch
tûnta pull
tútu mouse
TV ya n'singa cable TV

u (*e.g.*, **wu-**) it
ulembwa wânga deaf
Unio ya Europa European Union

vá on
vá mbela off, on the side
vá montele o'clock
vá nda far
vá nsi down
vá ntwala ntângu early
vá zulu (*prep.*) over, above
vákati among, in the middle
vakudila n'kalu deny
vâmbula ntâng'wa nda quarantine
vâna (*v.*) give, serve / (*adv.*) there; **lwâka vana**
  arrive there, at that place
váná (*adv.*) there; **wênda váná** go over there

vâna kiêse please, give or cause pleasure
vâna luve allow, permit, give permission
vâna mangwele vaccinate
vana mfuka (*v.*) loan, give a loan
vâna n'samu report, give news
vânda get initiation in obscure art like witchcraft or sorcery
vânga (*v.*) do, make, create
vângu (*n.*) tip
vangwa kia ndwanina arms, weapon
vanina kimbângi recommend, testify to
vaniye vanilla
vansi below
vantwâla before
vanwa luve allowed, be given permission
váta village
vâta dig with fingers or paws
vayika exit
vayika mênga bleed
vayika mu nswalu evacuate
vayikisa retrieve
vazulu top
ve no
vedila clean, proper
vêka (*v.*) rape
vêla glass
vêla ya matalatala lens
vêmbo shoulder
vento (*n.*) wind
vetile cab; car
via farm
via dia n'ti mia nkuna orchard
vididi lost

vidio video
vidisa lose
vilakana forget; ignore
Vilisi ya SIDA (VIH) HIV
vilusi virus
vîmbu blister
vinga (*v.*) alter, change
vingasa replace
vingila wait
visi bone
visi kia n'tu skull
viza visa
viza ya nkotila entry visa
vo if
vo dilendakane probably, if feasible, if possible
vola retrieve; withdraw
vônda kill, murder
vôti vote
vova pronounce, say, speak, utter
vovila declare
vukama (*v.*) assault
vûkisa rescue
vumu family; womb, abdomen
vûnga blanket
vunzangasa cancel
vutudila (*v.*) refund
vutukila repeat
vutula (*v.*) return
vutula m'funu fix
vutula mvutu reply
vuvama comfortable
vûvu (*v.*) trust
vuzanganwa ntima feel nauseous, nauseated

vuzangasa disturb
vuzangasa n'tima offend; cause nausea
vwa (*n.*) nine / (*v.*) own
vwalasi luggage
vwale veil
vwânda sit
vwândulu seat
vwâta (*v.*) dress, wear

wá listen
wâ hear
wa matiti desert
wa nienge desert
wa n'kento female
wa nkuna transplant
wa n'zôle (*adj.*) second (*ordinal number*)
wa vûvu reliable
wafwa dead
wafwema angry
wako cart
wako dia ndêkila sleeping car
wakolwa drunk
wakula adult
walembwa sômpa (*n.*) single
wamoyo alive
wandu chickpeas
wansiantima intimate
wena moyo (*n.*) person / (*adj.*) alive
wese kia babo public toilet
wîki honey
wiki wa ntulu cough syrup
winikina hear, listen, pay attention
wizana agree

wô all
wohama comfortable
wôla hour
wolele schedule
wôlo gold
wonsono all
wse kia bandônga public toilet
wûnu today

yá four
yà of
ya bandônga public (*of many people*)
ya bântu babo public (*of all people*)
ya fwa wrong; of broken; of dead
ya lumbu-ka-lumbu casual
ya mbantukulu original, of origin
ya mbudila bâdi stadium (for ball playing)
ya mfinda wild, of the forest
ya mun'tu mental
ya mvânun'wa wônga scary
ya m'vu annual
ya ndundila mbôngo bank account
ya n'nwa oral, by mouth
ya ntûla va baka mural on a wall
ya n'zôle (*n.*) second (*in time*)
yama spicy
yambila talk
yambula cancel
yamôko (*n.*) manual
yandaba hike
yandi mûnt'wa bakala he
yandi mûnt'wa n'kênto she
yangwa roasted

yanimosi alone
yantika start
yatiya (*adj.*) live
yawulu yogurt
ye and
ye bima bia nzo furnished
yêmba rob, steal
yêmbe pigeon
yêmbwa stolen
yênge happy
yengisa treat
yi lembwa mananga permanent
yidika mbokolo mu foni dial
yikamu kia tambi ankle
yimbila sing
yina that
yobila kwa dimuka bathe
yokwa kwa mwînia ntângu sunburn
yoluka cry
yongana have sex (*intercourse*)
Yuli July
yuma (*adj.*) dry
yumisa (*v.*) dry
yûnga coat
Yuni June
yuvula ask, question

zabibiôle double
zâka get
zala full
zându marketplace
zându dia bianteka flea market
zânga pool, basin, lake

zângi bean
zangula lift
Zavié January
zaya know
zaya diâka remember, know again
zayakanwa ordinary, be known
zayi knowledge
zayikisa warn
zayisa identify, let know
zekula (lusonso) screw
zekulwa kia lusonso screwdriver
zênga cut
zênga mangwele vaccinate
zênga nkanu decide
zênga nzevo shave
zengila tûmbu sentence (*legal*)
zêza loosen; melt
zi- they
ziakuta chew
zibula open, unlock
zibululu kia maza faucet
zidi face
zidi kia ndâmbu tatu triangle
zidi kia nsongolwa ntangu clock
ziêlo sand
ziêta travel
zîka bury
zikwa oven, stove
zimbazi za nzo (*n.*) outdoors
zindandulu za nzila nkwênda directions
zínga (*v.*) live
zînga (*v.*) wrap
zîngi (*adv.*) often, much, many

zingidisa delay
zinsadusulu amenities
zinsaka sports
ziôka hurry, run
ziôna kidnap
zisiki (*n.*) skis
zitisa (*v.*) respect
zitu (*adj.*) heavy / (*n.*) load
zo zoo
zodila vânga (*v.*) promise
zola (*v.*) like, love; want
zôle two
zôno yesterday
zônza (*v.*) dispute, argue
zúba (*v.*) pound, beat
zúlu altitude; sky
zulunale newspaper
zumbá (*n.*) sex (*intercourse*) / (*v.*) **tá zumbá** have
  sex/intercouse

ENGLISH-KIKONGO
DICTIONARY

abdomen vumu
able lenda
about fioti fisidi
above vá zulu
academy akademi
accelerator (*gas pedal*) akiselelatele (*pedale ya lesanzi*)
accent mvovolo
accept tambudila
access (*n.*) nkotolo
accident sumbula
accommodation ndekolo
account konti
accountant kontabele, n'tâng'ya mbôngo
accurate ibobo kibeni, ibuna kibeni
accusation mfundulu
accuse fúnda
acre (*0.4 hectares*) akele (*0.4 hekitale*)
across nsabukulu
act (*v.*) sála / (*n.*) nsalulu
activist kisadi
activity kisalu
actor n'sadi bimpa
actual bubu
add bundakasa
address (*n.*) adelesi, fulu kia nzingulu
administration luyâlu
admission ntambululu
admit tambudila
adult wakula, mbuta
advertisement ngialumusu, mbwangasa, pubilisite
after kuntwala, kunima
afternoon ku nima midi

again diâka
against n'tekwa nima
age mvula za nkudila
agency azanse
agent kisadi
agree wizana
agreement ngwizani
agriculture nsadul'wa mpatu
aid (*n.*) lusadisu / (*v.*) sadisa
aide (*n.*) n'sadisi
AIDS SIDA
air mupepe
air conditioning ntululu ya mupepe wa mbote
airline kompani dia ndeke, avio
airplane avio, ndeke
airport bânzala kia ndeke, fulu kia ndeke
airport tax mpaku ya bânzala kia ndeke
aisle divé
alarm ngûnga luzayisu
alcohol bitatila, lukolo
alive wamoyo, wena moyo; **be alive** kala môyo
all wonsono, wô
allergy fukutila
alley n'sâmba
allow vâna luve
allowed vanwa luve
almond alumondi
alone yanimosi
also diâka
altar mêza
alter soba, vinga
altitude zúlu, kayengele
aluminum foil papela ya aluminumu

always ntangu zazo
ambassador ntumwa luyalu
ambulance ambilasi
amenities zinsadusulu
among vákati
amount mbundakasu
and ye
anemic nkwa menga makuluka
anesthetic anesitetiki
angry wafwema, mu nganzi
animal búlu
ankle yikamu kia tambi
anniversary lumbu kia mvu wa mbutuka
announcement luzayisu
announcer n'zayisi
annoy tokanasa
annual ya mvu
antibiotics bilongo biantibiotiki
antifreeze antifrizi
antique kiankulu
antiseptic antisepitiki
any konso
anybody konso muntu
anyone konso muntu mosi
anything konso kima
anywhere konso kuma
apartment fulu kia masuku ma nzingila
apologize lômba nlevo, lômba ndoloki
apology ndoloki, ndodokolo, ndômbol'wa nlêmvo
appeal apele, kwenda kwa nsambisi wa zulu
appear monika bonso
appendicitis nsuka n'dia nene
appetite nzola dia

apple pomi
appointment lubwabwanu, mvanunu
apricot apilikoti
April Apila, Avili, Ngônda ya n'ya
architecture ntûngulu
area fulu
argue zônza
argument n'zonza
arm kima
arms (*weapons*) vangwa kia ndwanina
army kimakesa, alume
around mbela-mbela
arrival ndwakulu
arrest (*v.*) kânga, telamasa / (*n.*) nkangulu,
  ntelamasa
arrive lwaka
art arte, kinganga
arthritis mpasi za mianzi, ngalamatisi
artichoke alatisioke (unknown plant in Kongo area)
ash bombe, m'fututu wa tiya twa zima
ask yuvula, diá kiûvu
asleep kutolo, mandeka
aspirin asipirini, lóóngo kia nsadisila mpasi
assault (*v.*) vukama, takama / (*n.*) mvukama,
  ntakama
assist sadisa
assistant n'sadisi
associate (*n.*) n'koti mu kimvuka, mwesi kintwâdi /
  (*v.*) kota mu kimvuka
asthma nswengina, bêla kwa mfulumuna
ATM Masini ma Ntadila ye Mbakila Mbôngo
attack (*v.*) takama / (*n.*) ntakamu
attorney nzônzi ya min'siku, kivovi kia min'siku

August Agusita, Ngônda ya n'nana
author n'soniki
authority kimfumu
automatic otomatiki
automatic transmission talasimisio ya otomatiki
automobile ntomobilu
autumn otoni, nsung'ya nsotuka makaya
available sasuka, lenda sadilwa
avenue balabala, aveni
avoid lwênga, tîna
awake sikama
away kwanda
axle akise

baby mwâna nswa, n'sweswe, mpa
baby wipes masonia ma mwana nswa
babysitter ndezi (ya mwana)
back nima
backpack nsâku ya nima, nsâk'wa nima, sakodo
bad mbi, nkadi
bag nsâku
baggage kifunda
bakery nzo ya fûlu kia mampa
balcony balikoni
ball bâdi, somba
banana dinkondo dia n'koyongo
bandage tênda kia nkangila mputa
bank bânki, n'zwa ndundila mbôngo
bank account kônti ya banki, ya ndundila mbôngo
bar (*n.*) (*place for drinking*) siêlo, fulu kia ndwîna malavu
barber n'zêng'ya nsuki, n'tomis'ya zidi
barrel n'dungu

barrier nkakila
base sina
basement ndâmbu ya nzo ya sina, ns'ya ntoto
basin zânga, longa dia n'nene
basket kitunga
basketball bâdi dia kitunga
bat (*animal*) ngêmbo, mpuku-lu-nuni; (*sports equipment*) m'bota bâdi dia nzuba
bath ngyobila
bath towel sume ya ngiobidila
bathe yobila kwa dimuka
bathing suit m'vwatu wa ngiobidila
bathroom suku dia ngiobidila
battery bateli, n'kês'ya maza ma tiya
battle (*n.*) nkîndu, mvita
be (*v.*) kala (**am** ina; **is/are** ena; **was/were** kele, kedi, kezi, kezingi, kelenge; **been** ine, ena, eti + V-anga)
beach simu, kúmu
bean dêzo, zângi
beat (*v.*) zúba
beautiful mbote bêni
because diâmbu, mu diâmbu, kadi
because of mudiâmbu dia
become kituka
bed mfulu
bedding biamfulu
bedroom suku dia ndeka
bee ngiumbula; **bumblebee** fungununu
beef mbiz'ya ngômbe
beer biêle
before vantwâla, ntete
beggar nlômbi, kiyîngi

beginning mbantukulu, ngyantukulu
behind kunima
believe kwikila
bell ngûnga
below vansi, kunsi
berry mbuma
beverage mandwa
beware keba, lûka
bible bibila
bicycle bisikaleti, m'velo
big n'nene
bill n'kânda mfuka
birth certificate nkânda kimbângi kia mbutukila
birthday lumbu kia lubutuku
bite tatika
bitter ndudi
black ndômbe
blanket vûnga
bleed bûka mênga, vayika mênga
bless sâmbula
blind mpofo
blister vîmbu, buba
blood mênga
blood type kôndo wa mênga
blue bule
boarding pass nkânda mbântina mu ndeke, tiki
  kia bato
boat bato
body nitu
bomb bômbi, kindokila kia mpangula
bone visi
bonus m'vewo
book bûku

bookstore nzo ya n'kanda mia nteka, libeleli
boot bôti
border nzaku, nduta
bottle n'tûtu
bottom bându, nsi
box (*n.*) bwâti / (*v.*) tûla mu bwâti
boy mwâna bakala
boyfriend nkûnd'ya mwana bakala
brake (*n.*) fwele
bread dimpa
break mvûnda
breakfast diá kwa n'sûka
breathe (*v.*) fulumuna
bribe (*v.*) futa mboko
brick bidiki
bridge kiâmvu
bring kwiza nati
broken toluka, budika
brother nkazi, mpângi ya bakala ya se ye ngudi
  mosi
brown nkiena kulele ya titi kia yuma, kulele ya
  lukala lwa yuma
building ntûngulu
bull ngômb'ya bakala, koko
bullet kela
bumblebee fungununu
bureaucracy kikalaka
bury zîka, swêka mu ns'ya n'toto
bus bisi
bus terminal fulu kia nsukula ya bisi
business kisalu, bizinisi
busy kisalu mpasi
but kansi

butcher n'sâs'ya mbizi, kisâsi kia mbizi
butter manteka
button buto
buy sûmba

cab vetile, takisi
cabinet kobadi
cable n'singa
cable TV TV ya n'singa
café nz'wa kafi
cage mpaka
cake mukati, gato
calendar manaka
call (*v.*) bôkila / (*n.*) mbokolo
camera masini ma foto, sindima
camp fulu kia zinzo za mvwanda
campground n'toto wa zinzo zamvwanda
can *(modal verb)* lenda, kala ye ngangu, ngolo
cancel yambula, vunzangasa
candy bombo
car vetile
card kalati
carpet tapi
carrot kaloti
carry nata
carry-on biandata
cart wako
case (in this case) diâmbu, mu diâmbu; n'samu
cash (*v.*) baka mbôngo / (*n.*) mbakulwa ya mbôngo
casual ya lumbu-ka-lumbu
cat mbumba
catch (*v.*) takula, baka
cathedral nz'wa n'nene ya sambu

cattle bibulu bia ntwela, bitwelezi
cave suku dia tadi
cement sima
cemetery ndiamu, simitele
cent ndisu, santime
center kati-kati, santele
century nkama mvu
cereal seleyale
chain sieni
chair kiti
champagne sam'pani
change (*v.*) vinga, soba / (*n.*) mvinga, nsoba
changing room suku dia mvingila
channel kanale
chapel suku dia sambu, nsambidila
chapter kapu
charge (*n.*) nzitukulu
cheap mamvwemvwe, ntal'wa fioti
check (*v.*) talulula / (*n.*) ntalululu
checkpoint fulu kia ntalululu
cheese folomazi
chef mfumu ya bilambi, mfum'wa bilambi
chemical (*adj.* / *of chemical nature*) bia simi
chew nianguna, ziakuta
chicken nsusu
chickpeas wandu
chief (*adj.*) luta m'funu
child mwâna, kimwana-mwana
childcare kindezi kia mwâna
chocolate sokola
choke kakamana, swenwa
church nzwa Nzambi
cigarette sikaleti

cinema sindima
cinnamon sinamo
circle mvindumuka
citizen sitwaye
city mbânza
civilian mwesi nsi ya ngyala
clap sika nsiala, búla moko
class kalasi
classic kalasiki
clean vedila
client n'sûmbi
cliff nsuk'a benga
climate nsobol'wa kûma
climb mânta
clinic kiliniki
clock zidi kia nsongolwa ntangu, montele
close (*adj.*) batakana, finangana / (*v.*) kânga
closed kângama
cloth kitendi kia nlele
clothing min'lele, mimvwatu
club kîpi, kimvuka
clutch pedal pedale ya nsiensila ntînu
coat yûnga
cocoa kakawo
coconut nkândi ya kokoti
coffee kafi
coin sêngwa kia nzimbu
cold (*adj.*) kiakiozi / (*n.*) (*illness*) kiôzi kia bêla
collect kôngula, tôta
color maza ma, kulele ya
comb sanu
come kwîza
comedy mansevila

comfortable wohama, vuvama
commission lutumu, ntumunu
communication ntambukusu
companion nlândi
company kompani
compare swasikisa
compensation m'futu
complain tantala
complicated kiampimpita
compromise ngwizani, ngwawani
computer olidinatele
conceal swêka
concert n'kung'ya ngibila ye bisikwa
concrete kia nsimbikisa
concussion mbudika, ntêtuka
condom kapoti, kondomi, nkakila ya vumu kia
  mwana
conductor sofele, n'tambusi, kinati
conference ngiambila, ntel'wa mambu
conference room suku dia ngiambidila
confirm sikidika
constipated kângama kwa vumu, nkangama vumu
constitution luwawanu
consulate konsila
consul konsili, ntumwa luyalu lwa nzênza
contagious masambakanu
contraception mankakul'wa mbakul'wa vumu kia
  mwana
contraceptive lóóngo biankangila mabuta
contract luwizanu, kontala
convenience store makazini ma bima bianteka
convenient malukozamu
cook (*v.*) lamba

copy kopi
cord n'singa, mpangula
corn mbuma sangu
corner konko
correct (*adj.*) sungama
corrupt fwasakana, m'baki mia mboko
cosmetics kosimetiki
cost ntalu
cotton divunia
cough ntulu
cough syrup wiki wa ntulu
country nsi
country code kodi ya nsi
court nzo ya mfundusulu, tilibinale
courtesy mvwa luzitu
cover fuka
cover charge m'fut'wa mfuka
cream keleme, potopoto
create vânga
credit keledi, mbongu za mfuka
credit card kalati kia mfuka
crime sumu dia luyalu, mbi ya nsisi ya n'siku'wa
  luyalu
criticize someone kela
crowd ndônga
crutches minkawu mia mputu
cry sála/sá mazu, dila, yoluka
culture nkununu
cup kopo
cure kodidisa
curfew n'sik'wa ngemono mu mpîmpa
currency mbôngo zidiwanga mu nsi
currency exchange nsiensolo ya mbôngo

customer n'sûmbi
customs dwani
customs declaration mpovolo za dwani
cut zênga, bukuna

dairy madia ma kimvumina
damage mbebolo
dance makinu, kina
danger sumbula
dark tombe
date dati
date of birth dati ya mbutuka, lumbu kia mbutuka
daughter mwâna mbuta wa n'kento
dawn ntombe, mvunguka lumbu, nsûka
day lumbu
daytime ntang'wa mwini
dead kiafwa, wafwa
deadline nsuka ntangu
deaf m'fwe matu, ulembwa wânga
debt mfúka
decade kûmi dia m'vu
December Desemba, Ngônda ya kumi ye zole
decide zênga nkanu, baka nzengolo
decision n'kanu, n'zengo
deck bânzala kia bato
declare sâmbana, bôka, vovila
deep mvwamunu
delay zingidisa
delicious nsûnga
deliver (*of a baby*) búta; (*of goods*) sisa
delivery (*of a baby*) mbutulu
demand (*n.*) ndômbolo
democracy ngyadulu ya bantu kwa bantu

dentist ngânga ya meno
deny vakudila n'kalu
deodorant kia nkatudul'we nsudi
department store makazini ma n'nene ma bianteka
departure ndondokolo, nkatukulu
deposit mbôngo za nsîmbisa
depot fulu kia nsimbisila bima
desert n'zânza nkatu, wa matiti, wa nienge
desk bilo, mêza ma nsonikina
dessert biandia bia nsuka
destination fulu kia nsuka, kwe nsukina
detergent sabuni dia maza
diabetes diabeti
detour nzietokolo
diabetic nkwa diabeti
diagnosis mbonokon'we kimbêvo
dial yidika mbokolo mu foni
dialing code kodi ya mbokolo
diaper kûse ya mvwata
diarrhea nviôka vumu, pulu-pulu
dictate kâdila, têla
dictionary dikisionele
die fwa
diesel diezele
different swaswana
difficult mpasi
dig (*with fingers or paws*) vâta, (*with an instrument*) tima
dine diá
dining room suku dia ndîla
dinner diá kwa nkokila
diplomat ntumwa kinzonzi
direction ndandul'wa nzila

directions zindandulu za nzila nkwênda
directory buku dia zinkumbu
directory assistance lusalusu lwa buku dia
  zinkumbu
dirt doti
dirty kiadoti
disability mvânguka
disabled m'vânguki, nkwa kiêta
disagree lembwa wizana
disaster mvwalangani
discount nkulula
disease mayêla
dish lônga
display (v.) sôngisa
disposable kia ntuba
dispute (v.) zônza
district disitiliki, ndâmb'wa nsi
disturb vuzangasa
dive dimuka
dizziness nzûngana meso
dizzy n'zung'wa ntu
do sála, vânga
dock kúmu
doctor dokotolo, ngânga n'kisi
document dokima
dog mbwa
dollar dolale
domestic biamunzo
door kiêlo, kiavulu
double zabibiôle
dough mfûndi ya kwanga
down ku nsi, vá nsi
downtown ku n'dimba mbânza, ku vile

dozen nanga kûmi ye zôle
drain katula, benda
drama diantântu
drawer tilwale
dress (*n.*) m'vwât'wa fêti / (*v.*) vwâta
drink (*n.*) biandwa / (*v.*) nwa
drive nata (n'tomobilu)
driver's license pelemi ya ndatun'wa ntomobilu
drown dimuka
drowsy mêso zungana
drug bilôngo
drugstore makazini ma bilongo, falamasi
drunk wakolwa
dry (*adj.*) yuma / (*v.*) yumisa
dry cleaner n'sukudi wa masini ma ngyumisina
dryer masini ma ngyumisina
dust (*v.*) katula pusiele
duty-free kóndwá kwa futa dwane
dye tûla maza ma kulele

ear kútu
earache ntatikwa kutu, ndûnza kutu
early vá ntwala ntângu
earth n'toto
earthquake nzakama n'toto
east kuvaikilanga ntangu, esiti
eat diá
economy ndundulu ya bisalu, mbutul'wa mbôngo
education ndongolo, nsansulu
egg diâki
eight nâna
eighteen kûmi-ye-nâna
eighty lunâna

election nsôlolo
electric kiakulan
electricity kulan
elevator asansele
eleven kûmi-ye-mosi
e-mail emele
embassy ambasade, nz'wa ntumwa luyalu lwa nzênza
emergency dia nswâlu, dia nzaki
emergency room suku dia lusadisu lwa nswâlu, suku dia nzáki
employee kisadi
employer m'vwe, mfum'wa kisalu
empty nkatu, mpamba
end nsuka
enemy mbêni
energy (ngolo za)tiya
engine motele
engineer enzeniele, ngânga n'sadi
English language kingelezo
engraving mantima
enough fwâna
enter kota
entertainment nsakanasa
entire m'vîmba
entrance mwêl'wa nkotila
entry nkotolo
entry visa viza ya nkotila
envelope mvolopo
epileptic kimanga, nkisi wa (ki)teke, kipupa
equal fwanana
equipment kisalulwa
escalator kimantunu kia sikalie

estimate tezikisa
ethnic kisi kanda
Europe / European Union (Ns'ya) Mputu
European Mputuki, Mwesi mputu
evacuate vayika mu nswalu
even mpila mosi
evening nkokila
event n'samu
eventually kukwiza ntangu
ever m'vu ye m'vu, ntângu yi lembolo manu
every konso
exact ibubu, ibobo, ibuna kibeni
examine toma tala
example nsongisa, mbându
except katula kaka
excess kilutidi
exchange soba
exchange rate ntalu ya nsobolo
exclude katula
exhaust manisa
exhibit (*v.*) sôngisa / (*n.*) nsongosolo
exit vayika, mvayikulu, mwêlo
expense mfutulu, nsalul'wa mbôngo
expensive ntalu mpasi, ntal'wa ngolo
experience nzayilu
expiration date lumbu kia nsuka
explain sâsila
export nata ku nsia n'kaka
express mu nswâlu bêni
express train lukâlu lwa nswâlu
extra sundidi
eye disu
eyeglasses nguya, matala-tala

fabric nlele wa ntunga
face zidi, luse
fall bwa
false kaludi ko
family dibuta, vumu
famine n'satu
far kwa nda, vá nda
fare tiki
farm via, mpatu, fulu kia nsansila bibulu
fast (*adj.*) ntînu, n'swâlu
fast food madia ma ntînu, madia ma nswâlu
fat mafuta, mazi
father se, tata, m'buti wa bakala
faucet lobinet, kangulu kia maza, zibululu kia maza
fax (*n.*) fakisi / (*v.*) fidisa fakisi
February Fevilie, Ngônda ya nzole
fee mbôngo za mfuta
feel mona mu nitu
female wa n'kento
fence lupângu
ferry masuwa, bat'wa bantu
festival n'kûngi
fever mazunu
field fulu kia zibuka
fifteen kûmi-ye-tanu
fifty makum'matanu
fig m'filu
fill fulusa
film filime
find solula
finger nlêmbo
fire tiya

fire alarm ngûnga nzayikuswa tiya
firewood nkuni
fireworks bindokila bia tiya, miletwale
first ntete
first-aid kit nkutu ya lusadisu lwa ntete
first-class kalasi kia ntete
fish mbizi ya maza, n'koko
fisherman n'takudi, n'yabi wa mbizi za maza
fishing ntakula, ngyabul'wa mbizi za maza
fishing license luvê lwa ntakudila
fishing permitted (*phrase*) takula kuvanunu luve
fishing rod n'ti ye n'singa ntakudila
fist nkome
fit (*v.*) fwâna
fitting fwanisa
fitting room suku dia ntezolo
five tânu
fix vutula m'funu
flag dalapo
flame n'laku
flare nsezemo
flash mwînda
flash photography foto ya mwînda
flashlight mwînda tolose
flat kiadôka
flat tire pine ya dôka
flavor ntomo, nsûnga
flea kinsekwa, nsombukila, n'tanda
flea market zându dia bianteka
flight ntilumuka
flight number nomba ya ntilumuka
flood mfuluka n'koko, kizalu
floor n'tot'wa nzo

flour fufu
flourish toma kula
flower fololo, mfula
flu fukutila, mazunu
fluent nzaki
fluid kia maza
flush benda maza
fly (*v.*) tilumuka / (*n.*) (*insect*) niânzi, kimfwetete
fog bûngi, m'bungisi
folk kibuti, mpângi
folk art bisalu bia besi nsi, kinganga kia besi nsi
follow lânda
food ndia, madia, bidia
food poisoning ndikidila ya madia
foot tâmbi
football (*soccer*) bâdi, bâle dia mâlu, sombala
footpath n'sâmba, nzila mâlu
forehead mbûnzu
foreigner nzênza
foreign currency mbôngo za nzênza
foreign languages ndînga nzênza
forest mfînda
forget vilakana
forgive lemvukila
fork n'soma
formal kia lukofi, kia mâvu
fortune kimvwâma
fortuneteller m'bikud'ya mambote
forty makum'maya
fountain n'kelo
four yá
fourteen kûmi-ye-ya
fraud ngyêmba, bwîvi

free kóndwá futila, mpovo
freeze kânga mu kiôzi
fresh n'twênia, mpa
Friday (Lumbu) Kiatânu, Kian'tânu
friend n'kûndi
front luse, n'twâla
front desk bilo kia nkotolo, ngyambulu
frozen kângama kwa kiôzi
fruit mbuma n'ti
fry kânga mu mafuta
fuel (*for starting a fire*) bia ndemosolo tiya
full fuluka, zala
fun (*n.*) kiêse / **have fun** (*v.*) mona kiêse
funeral bêndo
funny dianseyila
furnished ye bima bia nzo
furniture bima bia mvwânda ye lêkila
future kuntwâla, kunima, ku kukwîza ntângu

game nsaka
garden (*n.*) fimpatu fia bia nkuna
gas tank lezevwale ya lesanze
gasoline lesanze, maza matiya
gear sanzema ya ntînu
general mu mawonso
get baka, zâka
gift kiankayilwa
girl mwâna ndûmba, kindende kia nkênto
girlfriend ndûmba nzolwa
give vâna
glass vêla
glasses (eyeglasses) ngûya.matala-tala
glue kôlo

go kwênda
goat nkômbo
gold wôlo
good mbote
goods n'solo
gossip kela
government luyâlu
gram galame
grammar galamele, n'kânda ndînga
grandchild n'tékólo
grandfather n'kâka bakala
grandmother nkâka n'kênto
grape mbuma za nzenzo
grass pasipalomi, matîti
great mbote bêni
green maza ma niâza
greeting (kia) mbote
grocery store makazini ma biandia
ground (*n.*) n'toto / (*adj.*) fusakana
group n'kângu
guard (*n.*) n'kengedi, sinzidi / (*v.*) kengila
guest nzênza
guide (*n.*) n'tâmbusi
guidebook bûkua dia ntwadisi
guilty n'tambudid'ya mambi
gun n'kele
gym suku dia ndikuzun'wa nitu

hair nsuki
half ndambu a kati-kati
hall suku dia n'nene dia nzo
halt nîngama
hand kôko

handicapped nkwa kiêta
happiness (*n.*) kiêse / **feel happiness** (*v.*) mona kiêse
happy yênge
harass tokanasa
harbor kúmu
hard ngolo
harm mbi
hat mpu
hazard kia sumbula
he yandi mûnt'wa bakala
head n'tu
health nkodila
health insurance nsikidis'wa nkodila
hear wâ, winikina
heart n'tima
heart attack nkangama n'tima
heat ndungutila
heavy zitu
hello (*to an individual*) kiambote kiaku, (*to more than one person*) kiambote kieno, mbote, (*interj.*) enge, nge
help lusadisu
herb tîti
here eva, eku, emu
heterosexual n'zod'ya matoko ye bandumba
hey (*interj.*) nge, enge
hide swêka
highway nzila ntomobilo
hike yandaba
hill kimongo-mongo
HIV Vilisi ya SIDA (VIH)
hole n'wa, búlu

holiday mvûnda
holy kiasântu
home nz'wa mvwânda
homeless munkondwa nzo
homosexual mûnt'wa bakala nkwa ntok'wa
  babakala
honest mûntwa ludi
honey wîki
honeymoon ngônda wîki kwa toko ye ndûmba
horse mpûnda, m'vâlu
hospital lupitalu
hospitality n'gyambul'wa bântu, ntambudul'wa
  bântu
hostage n'kangami wa kingolo
hostel finzo fia ndêka mviokolo
hostile kóndwá kwa nzola
hot tiya twa ngyoka
hotel nz'wa ndêka ya mviokolo
hour wôla, mu wôla
house nzo
how bwe(yi)
hug bûmba
human bumûntu
human rights maluvê ma bumûntu
hundred nkama
hunger n'satu
hunt saka
hunter nkongo, m'vond'ya bibulu
hurry n'swâlu, ziôka, nzaki
hurt lwâla
husband bakala dia n'sômpi, n'kaz'ya bakala

ice maza makangama kwa kiôzi

ID card kalati kia nzayil'wa muntu
idea ngîndu, bânza
identification nzayil'wa muntu
identify zayisa
idiom dia ta bambuta
if vo, nga vo, ndio, nga ndio
ignite kwîka, tûla tiya
ignore vilakana, ku landi ko
illegal dia n'siku, dia kondwa luve
illness bêla, kimbêvo
immigrant mungizila, n'tangumuki
immigration kingizila, ntangumuka
impolite kóndwá kwa luzitu
import nkotisa, mbokolo ya bima mu nsi
improve tomisa
income mbakul'wa mbôngo
incorrect lembwa sungama, ka bwa(wu) ko, ka
  bobo ko
individual kia (mûntu) yandi mosi
indoor mu kati dia nzo
inexpensive mamvwemvwe, ka ntalu ya yingi ko
infant kimwana-mwana
infect tambukisa
infected tambakane
infection ntambakani
influence sokisa
influenza fukutila
information nsângu
information desk bilo kia nsângu
infrastructure mantungul'we nsi
inject kotisa
injury mvânguka
ink tînta

inn nz'wa mvundila
innocent munkond'wa diambu
inquiry kiûvu
insect kintudimoya
insect bite tatikul'wa kia ma kiamôya
insect repellant n'kum'ya kintudimoya
inside mukati
inspect toma tala
instant fintângu
institution ntûngulu
insufficient lembwa fwâna
insulin insilina
insult fîngu
insurance insulansi
international bia zinsi zanza
Internet Inteleneti
interpret sekula mambu
interpretation nsekodol'wa mâmbu
interpreter n'sekod'ya mâmbu
intersection mpâmbu
intimate wansiantima
introduce oneself kisongisa, kikotisa
intruder n'koti ya kimwîvi
invite bôkila
iron sêngwa
irritate tokanasa, fwêmisa
island sânga
issue diâmbu
it i, u (*e.g.* di-, ki-, or wu-)
itch mfisima
item kima
itinerary nzila

jacket n'zâka
jail boloko
jam (*fruit condiment*) potopoto; (*traffic*) nkakila
January Zavié, Ngônda ya ntete
jar fikopo
jeans m'bat'ya zini
Jew Hebeleo
jewelry bidîngwa
job kisalu
join kota, kângama ye
journalist n'soniki
judge (*v.*) (*leg.*) n'sambisi, fûndisa
jug nkalu
juice maza ma mbuma
July Yuli, Ziyé, Ngônda ya nsambwadi
jump dumuka
jumper cables n'singa mia nsambudila tiya
junction ngikamu
June Yuni, Zwen, Ngônda ya nsambanu
jungle mfînda nkobo
just kaka
justice bunsôngi

keep (*v.*) lûnda
kettle mbidika
key nsabi
kick (*v.*) búla
kid mwâna
kidnap ziôna
kidney mfiângu
kill vônda
kilogram kilogrami
kilometer kilometa

kind mpila
kiss fiba
kit bisalulwa
kitchen kikûku
knapsack nkutu
knee kinkoso
knife kotika, mbele
knit tûnga
knock konkutila
knot kólo
know zaya
knowledge zayi
kosher kibeni

lady ndûmba, n'kênt'wa luzitu
lake zânga
lamb même
lamp mwînda
land n'toto
lane mwâlu
language ndînga
laptop laputopi
large n'nene
last nsuka
late landidila
later kweyele ntângu
laugh seva
laundromat nz'wa nsukudila nlele
laundry nlele mia nsukula
lavatory kiobila, dusi
law n'siku
lawyer kivovi, nzônzi ya minsiku
layover nîngama

leader mvitia n'tu
leaf lukaya
league kimvuka
learn longuka
leather kwîle
leave katuka
left katukidi
leg kûlu
legal kia n'siku
legislature nsadul'wa min'siku
lemon lâla dia nsa
lens vêla ya matalatala
less fiôti, luta buke
letter letula, n'kânda
lettuce ndûnda leti
level nivo
library nzo ndundila mabuku
lice nianzi za n'tu
license lisansi
lid batukwa, kifinuku
lie luvunu
life luzingu
lift zangula, tombula
light mwînda
lighting nkwikul'wa mwinda
lightning nsezemo
like (*v.*) zola / (*prep.*) nkiena, bônso
lime tadi
limit (*v.*) sukisa / (*n.*) nsuka
lip koba
liquid maza
liquor bitatila, malavu mangolo
list nlonga

listen wá, winikina
liter litele
litter fwasikisa
little fiôti
live (*v.*) zínga / (*adj.*) yatiya
liver nsoko
lizard kidiasala
load (*v.*) soka, tûla / (*n.*) zitu
loaf kwânga
loan (*n.*) mfúka, nsômpa / (*v.*) devisa, vana mfúka
lobby suku dia ngyambidila
local disuku
location fulu
lock kânga mu kumba
lock out kangidila
locker kobadi dia kumba
long ndâ
look tala
loosen zêza
lose vidisa, pola
lost vididi, polele
lounge fulu kia ndîla
love (*n.*) nzola / (*v.*) zola
low munsi
lucky mu lawu
luggage kifunda, vwalasi
lunch diá kwa mwini

machine masini
mad lawuka
maid nlâmbi a nkênto
mail (*n.*) (mi)n'kânda / (*v.*) fila nkânda mu posita
main (*adj.*) sunda biabio

make (*v.*) sála, vânga
man mûnt'wa bakala wakula
mandatory fweti, kóndwá kwa nsola
manual (*n.*) yamôko
many biabîngi, zîngi
map kalati kia n'toto
March Malasi, Ngônda ya ntatu
marketplace zându
marriage nsompani
married kwelele
marry kwêla
massage niemangasa, bwêta
math ntalu
mattress matalasi
maximum mfuluka nsuka
May Mayi, Ngônda ya n'tanu
meal madia
measure mesile, ntezakasa, têzo
meat mbizi
mechanic mekaniki
medication bilôngo
medicine lóóngo, n'kisi, bilôngo
medium (*adj.*) mbela kati
meet (*v.*) bwabwana
meeting mbwabwani
melon lenge
melt zêza
member ndâmbu ya
menstruation mvayika menga ma bukento
mental ya mun'tu
menu meni
merchant n'kiti
message n'samu

messenger n'natia nsamu, ntumwa
metal sêngwa
meter metele
metro station stasio ya metolo, nzila ns'ye ntoto
microwave mikolonde
midday midi, ntângu va mbata n'tu
middle kati
midnight n'dingu wa nsi, kati dia mpimpa
might ngolo
migraine m'bwangu wa ntu
mild kati-kati
mile mîle
military kisoda
milk kimvumina
million kiâzi
mine (*pron.*) kiâmi, kia mono
minimum ndwêlo ya nsuka
minor (*adj.*) fiôti / (*n.*) kindende
mint bulukutu
minute miniti
mirror kitalatala, pêlo
misunderstanding mvwalangani, kóndwá kwa
  mbakusulu
mix balula
mobile phone fôni mobile
moment fintângu
Monday Kiamonde, Kialendi
money mbôngo
monkey nkewa
month ngônda
monument kifwâniswa, kiteke kia n'nene
moon ngônda
more (*adv.*) lutila, sundila

morning nsûka
mosque mosike, nz'wa nzambi ya mizilima
mosquito lubu
mosquito net musitikele
most (*adv.*) kisundidi biabio
motel motele, fihotele
mother ngudi
mother-in-law nzit'wa nkênto
motion sickness bêla kwa nzietolo, nikuzuka
motor motele
motorcycle moto
mount mantisa, tûla va zulu
mountain môngo
mouse tútu
moustache masunia
mouth n'nwá
move (*v.*) nikuka, ningana, bênduka
movie sindima
movie theater teatele ya sindima
Mr. (*title*) Mesie, Tâta, Mbuta
Mrs. (*title*) Madami, Mâma
Ms. (*title*) Mama mwâna nkêto, Mama fiôti
much fwâna, mbidi, zîngi
mud nteke, poto-poto
mural ya ntûla va baka
murder vônda
muscle n'suni
museum mizé
mushroom luwa
music miziki
musical instrument salulwa kia miziki, sikulwa
   kia miziki
musician m'bud'ye miziki

Muslim Mizilima
mystery mpimpita, ngitukulu bêni

naked mpeni, mwâsi
name nkûmbu
napkin kitendi kia n'nwa, papela ya nkusunina n'nwá
narrow swênga, siôka
nation besi nsi
native butukila
nature nzâ
nausea (*n.*) n'sat'wa luka / (*v.*) **cause nausea** vuzangasa n'tima; **feel nauseous** vuzanganwa ntima
navigation nsônga nziêtolo va nsi, navigasio
navy kisoda kia maza ma n'nene
near mbela
nearby mbela-mbela
neck nsîngu
necklace n'sânga
need (*v.*) kala ye m'funu / (*n.*) nsat'wa ngolo
needle ntûmbu
neighbor m'batakani
neighborhood mbati-mbati
nephew mwâna nkazi wa bakala
nerve mwânzi
neutral kôndwa-ndâmbu
never (*adv.*) kani-nkutu, ka nsa mosi nkutu ko
new mpa
New Year Mv'wa mpa, Mvula mpa
New Year's Day Lumbu kia Bwanana, Lumbu kia ntete kia mvu
New Year's Eve Nkokila yi vitanga, tekilanga m'vwa mpa

news nsângu
newspaper zulunale, nkânda nsângu
next lândila
next to lândila va nima
nice mbote
niece mwâna nkazi wa nkêto
night mpîmpa, ntâng'wa tômbe
nightlife luzingu lwa mpîmpa
nine vwa
nineteen kûmi-ye-vwa
ninety luvwa
no ve, nkatu, ka bwa(u) ko
noise mâzu
non-smoki1ng lembwa nwînwa fûmu
noodles nuye (*from French "nouilles"*)
noon midi, ntângu va mbata n'tu
normal busadilwanga
north nolo, ntand'wa nsi
northeast nolo-esita
northwest nolo-wesita
nose mbômbo
note nôti
nothing ka lekwa ko, ka kima ko
November Novemba, Ngônda ya kumi ye mosi
now bubu
nowhere ka kûma ko
nuclear nukilele
nudist beach simu dia bankwa mpeni
number nomba, numolo
nun mamêla, masêla
nurse m'fwelemi
nuts nkândi

occupant mwesi-nzo, mwesi fulu, m'vwa fulu
occupation kisalu
ocean kalunga, m'bu
o'clock vá montele
October Okutoba, Ngônda ya n'kumi
octopus ntentemb'wa maza, pievele (non-Kôngo)
odor nsudi
of yà
off (*adv./adj.*) vá mbela
offend lwêka, vuzangasa n'tima
office bilo
officer kalaka, kisadi kia bilo
official dia nwa kimfumu
often (*adv.*) nkumbu za mbidi, zîngi
oil mafuta
OK Ibobo, diwizanono
old nunu, mbuta
olive mungenge
on vá
once nkumbu mosi, nsa mosi
one mosi
one-way nzila nkwênda mosi
onion niâza
only kaka
open zibula
opera opela (*non-Kôngo*)
operator kisadi
opposite ndâmb'wa n'ka, sâmbu dia n'ka
option nsôlolo
or evo
oral ya n'nwa
orange lala dia n'zênzo
orchard via dia n'ti mia nkuna

orchestra olukesita (*non-Kôngo*)
order lutumwa, nsungikilu
ordinary zayakanwa
organ kisikwa, olugani (*non-Kôngo*)
organic kimenina kia n'toto
original ya mbantukulu
other n'kaká
ought fweti
our êto
out (*adv.*) kumbazi
outdoor (*adj.*) kumbaz'ya nzo
outdoors (*n.*) zimbazi za nzo
outside kumbaz'ya nzo
oven fûlu, zikwa
over (*prep.*) vá zulu
overdose kolwa
overnight (*adv.*) mpîmpa mvîmba
own (*v.*) vwa
owner (*n.*) m'vwe
oxygen okisizeni

pack paki, fûnda
package fûnda
page paze, lukaya
paid futwa, futulu
pain mpasi; **feel pain** mona mpasi
painful mona mpasi
painkiller kodidisa mpasi
pair biôle
pajamas pizama, m'vwât'we ndêkila
pan nzûngu
pants m'bati
paper papela

parcel fifûnda
pardon (*n.*) nlêmvo / (*v.*) lenvukila
parent m'buti
park (*n.*) paleke / (*v.*) telemasa
parking ntelamasa, fulu kia ntelamasa ntongobilu
parliament nz'wa kinzonzi
partner makângu, n'kûnd'ya luzingu, kisalu
party (*celebration*) n'kûngi, (*political*) kimvuka
passenger n'ziêti
passport pasepolo
password modepase
pasta pâti, mfûndi
pastry kiapâti
path n'sâmba, mwâlu
patience luvibudulu
patient (*n.*) mbêvo
pavement n'tôt'we simenta
pay futa
payment mfutulu
pea ndambá
peace luvuvamu
peach pitsi
peak (*top of*) mbata
peanuts nguba
pedal pedale
pedestrian n'tambudi, n'diâti
pen sonokono kia tinta
penalty tûmbu
pencil lapi
people bântu
pepper ndûngu
percent pulusa
perfect mbot'ya nsuka

period nsûngi

permanent lumbu-ka-lumbu, m'vu-ye-m'vu, yi lembwa mananga

permission luvê; **give permission** vâna luvê

permit (*v.*) vâna luvê / (*n.*) luvê

person muntudimoya, wena moyo

personal mûntu-mosi

pest bwêle kiambi

pet (*n.*) bwêle kianzo

petrol (*gas*) lesanzi, (*kerosene*) pitiloya

pharmacy falamasi, makazini ma bilôngo

phone fôni; **public phone** fôni ya bântu babo, fôni ya bandônga; **mobile phone** fôni mobile

phone booth kabini ya fôni

phone card kalati kia fôni

phone number nomba ya fôni, numolo ya fôni

photograph foto, kimazi, kifwâniswa

phrase diâmbu dia mvîmba

physician ngânga bilongo

piano piano

pick up bônga, tôta

picnic dia-kwa-paleke

picture kifwâniswa, kimazi

pie kênde

piece tini

pig ngulu

pigeon yêmbe

pill mbuma

pillow kus'ya (ntûla)ntu

pint pinta

pipe (*for tobacco*) su; (*for water*) tiyo

place fulu

plain kimona-mêso

plan diena-salulwa
plane ndeke, avio
plant kimenina
plastic kapala
plate longa-dia-yalumuku
platform fulu-ki-mvovila
play (*n.*) nsaka / (*v.*) sakana
pleasant kiêse
please vâna kiêse
plug fulu kia kula
pocket posi
poem pweme
point pwe
poison maswa, pwazo
police pulisi
police station bilo kia pulisi
polite kia-luzitu
politics politiki
pollution mbêbisa
pool zânga
population ndônga
pork mbiz'ya ngulu
portable lênda natwa, kiandata
possibly lendakane
post office bilo-kia-posita
postage mfidusulu mu posita
postal code kodi ya posita
postbox bwati-ya-posita, nkela ya posita
postcard kalati-kia-posita
postpone fila ku-ntwala, fila mu ntang'wa kunima
pot kînzu
potato mbala, mbumbulutela
pottery bikinzu

pound (*n.*) pandu / (*v.*) zúba
pour sekula, tiamuna
poverty bumputu, kóndwá kwa mbakulwa
power ngolo
pray sâmbila
prefer luta, sunda zola
pregnant kala ye vumu (kia mwana); **become pregnant** kokama
prescription n'kânda bilôngo
president mfum'we luyalu, mfum'we nsi, pelezida
price ntalu
priest ngânga nzâmbi
printer empirimante, masini ma bisono
prison boloko
prisoner mûnt'wa boloko, n'kangami
privacy bunswêki, bwamûntu mosi
private kinswêki, kia mûntu mosi
private property kimvwe kia kinswêki, kia mûntu mosi
private room suku dia kinswêki
prize m'futu
probably vo dilendakane
problem diâmbu dia mpasi
product m'butu
professionalism nzayil'wa kisalu
professor nlông'ya kalasi kia zulu
profile mbonokono
profit nluta
program mansadila, pologalami
prohibit tûla n'siku
project mena salua
promise (*v.*) zodila vânga / (*n.*) mena vangwa
promotion mbiêkolo

pronounce vova
proper vedila, mpwênia
property mvwîlu
prosecute tûmba
prosecution ntûmbulu
protect kebila
protest mpaka
Protestant Misioni, Mfid'ya mpaka
province polovinse, tini kia ns'ya luyâlu
psychologist ngânga nkalulu, ngânga bifu
public (*adj.*) (*of all people*) ya bântu babo, (*of many people*) ya bandônga
public telephone fôni ya bântu babo, fôni ya bandônga
public toilet wese kia babo, wse kia bandônga
public transportation ndatunu ya babo
pull tûnta, benda
pulse nsálul'wa ntima
pump (*n.*) pompi / (*v.*) pompa
punch bânda nkomi
puncture tobula
punish tûmba
purchase sûmba
pure mpwênia
purple fumfu
purpose m'funu
purse polotefe
push tîndika, pusa
puzzle mpitakani
pyramid pilamidi

qualify sôngila mfunu
quality fu kiambote

quantity kûnku, (*of something like meat*) budi
quarantine vâmbula ntâng'wa nda
quarter ndâmbu mosi ya n'ya
queen n'tin'wa nkênto
query kiûvu
question (*v.*) yuvula, diá kiûvu / (*n.*) ngyúvu
queue n'lông'e nda
quick nzaki, n'swâlu, ntînu
quiet napî, kondwa mâzu evo ndingana

radio ladio
rail nlayi
railroad nzila n'layi, nzila bisêngwa
rain (*n.*) mvula / (*v.*) noka
ramp nzila lukongolo
rape (*n.*) mvelula / (*v.*) vêka
rapid mu nswâlu
rare mpasi mu mona, baka
rat mpuku
rate nivo
ratio lasio
ration lasio
raw nkûnzu
razor luzwâlu, lazwâle
read tânga
ready sikila
rear nima
reason bila
reasonable nkalul'wa bila
rebel nkwa lulêndo, lebele, n'nwanis'ya luyâlu
rebellion kimvuka kia bankwa lulendo, lebelio
receipt nkânda kimbângi
receive baka, tâmbula

recognize tambudila
recommend vanina kimbângi
record kânga
rectangle lekitangele
recycle futumuna
red mbwâki
referee (*n.*) m'fûndisi / (*v.*) fûndisa
reference kimbângi
refrigerator filigo
refuge swâmunu, fulu kia nswamina
refugee lefizé, n'swâmi
refund (*v.*) vutudila / (*n.*) mvutudila
regime lezime, mpila luyâlu
region ndâmbu, tini kia nsi
registration nsonokono
regular busadilwânga
relationship kikûndi, kimpângi
relative mpângi
reliable kia lukwikilu, wa vûvu
religion mambu ma Nzâmbi
remedy (*n.*) bilôngo
remember bambukila, zaya diâka
remind bâmbula ntima
remove katula
rent (*v.*) futila / (*n.*) mbôngo za mfutila nzo
repair tomisa
repair shop nz'wa ntomosono
repay futa
repayment mfutulu, mvutudulu
repeat vutukila
replace vingasa
reply vutula mvutu
report lapolo, vâna nsamu

reporter m'vâni a nsamu, n'twâdi a n'samu, matwâdi
republic lepibilike
request (*v.*) lômba / (*n.*) ndômbolo
require fweti
rescue vûkisa, mvûkisa
reservation ndundulu
reserve ndundila
reservoir ma kia ndundila
respect (*n.*) luzitu / (*v.*) zitisa
rest mvûnda
restaurant nz'wa ndîla
restricted (*adj.*) kia bansôla, kia biansôla
resumé/resume bunkufi, bantika diâka
retrieve vola, vayikisa
return (*v.*) vutula / (*n.*) mvutuka
reverse balula
revive futumuna
revolution mvinga ngolo
rib lubânzi
ribbon kitêndi
rice lôso
ride mânta
right (*adj.*) sûngama / (*n.*) nsûngama, luvê
ring (*n.*) (*jewelry*) nêla; (*sound*) ngûnga / (*v.*) búla ngûnga
riot nkîndu, mvita
rip tiâba
risk sumbula
river n'kóko, nzadi
road nzila n'nene
road map kalati kia nzila
roasted yangwa

rob yêmba
robber mwîvi
rock (*n.*) tadi / (*v.*) dungasa, nikuna mu ngolo
romance kindûmba, kitoko
romantic dia kindûmba, kitoko
roof nludi
room suku
room rate ntal'wa suku
room service ndatun'wa madia mu suku
rope n'singa
rot bola
rotten kiabola
rough mfwankayi
round-trip kwênda-vutuka
round-trip ticket tiki kia kwênda-vutuka
route nzila
royalty luzitu lwa kimfumu
rubber kawusu
rude kôndwá luzitu
rug fitapi
rugby lugibi, nsaka za badi dia ndwanina
ruins mfûka, bisisulwa
rule n'siku
run ziôka

sacred kisântu
sad kiâdi
saddle kiti kia mpûnda, kiti kia mvelo, moto
safe kia luvuvamu
safety luvuvamu
sail pûswa kwa mupepe va ntand'wa maza
salad ndûnda salata
salary m'fut'wa kisalu mu mbôngo

sale ntekolo
sales receipt nkânda ntekolo
sales tax mpak'wa ntekolo
salon suku dia ngyambidila
salt mûngwa
same mpila mosi
sample kifwâniswa
sanction tûmbu
sanctuary nz'wa sâmbu, nzo ya nzâmbi, nz'wa nzâmbi
sand ziêlo
sandals sandale
sandwich sandwisi
sanitary napkin muswalu wa mavimpi
satellite sateliti
Saturday Kiasabala
sauce sosi
sausage sosaze
save lûnda
saw (*n.*) n'kwânga
say vova, tá
scanner sikanele
scar fu kia mputa
scare mwîsa wônga
scarf fulale
scary ya mvânun'wa wônga
scene kimpa
scenery kimpa kia nsi
schedule wolele, nsadul'wa ntângu
school sikulu
science sianse, nsosolo a ngângu ye ndwênga
scissors sizo
score (*n.*) kôngo / (*v.*) tûla kôngo

screen ekala
screw zekula (lusonso)
screwdriver zekulwa kia lusonso
sculpture kifwâniswa kianzoka (mun'ti evo mu tadi)
sea m'bu
seafood madia ma m'bu
seam mviba
search (*n.*) nsosolo / (*v.*) sosa
seasick bêla kwa mvuzangana ntima mu m'bu
season (*of a year*) nsûngi
seasonal (*of a year*) bia nsungi, kia nsûngi
seasoning (*for food*) biansûnga, ntululu ya biansûnga
seat vwândulu
seat belt sentile ya kiti
seat number nomba ya mvwândulu
second (*n.*) (*in time*) ya n'zôle, ntângu / (*adj.*)
   (*ord. num.*) wa, kia n'zôle
secondhand store makazini ma tombola
secret dia sekele, ma kinswêki, sekele
secretary sekeletele
section kitini, sekisio
secular ma kisi n'tôto, kia kisi n'tôto
security luvuvamu
sedative ma n'kululul'wa mpasi, mia n'kululul'wa
   mpasi
see mona
seed mbuma za nkuna
seek sosa
seem bônso
select (*v.*) sôla
selection nsôla
self-service kisadisa
sell teka

seminar ndongokolo za mâmbu

senate sena

senator senatele, kisadi kia minsiku

send fila

senior mfumu

sensitive dia ngengesi

sentence (*gram.*) nlônga diâmbu, falaze; (*legal*) zengila tûmbu

separate (*adj.*) (*of separate nature*) dia kabana, bia kabana / (*v.*) kabula

September Sepitemba, Ngônda ya m'vwa

serious dia ngolo, mpasi

servant mu mvanunu

serve vâna

server m'vâni

service mvanunu

settlement ntûngulu

seven nsambwadia

seventeen kûmi-ye-nsambwadi

seventy lusambwadi

sew tûnga

sex (*n.*) (*of female gender*) kikênto, (*of male gender*) kibakala; (*intercourse*) zumbá / (*v.*) **have sex** tá zumbá, yongana

shampoo siampu, sabuni dia maza mu sukula nsuki

share kabula, kabana

shark ngo maza

sharp nsôngi

shave zênga nzevo, katula nzevo

shaving cream keleme ya manzevo

she yandi mûnt'wa n'kênto

sheep même

sheet dala
shellfish munsala
shelter n'sâmpa, fulu kia mvûndila
ship masuwa, bato
shirt kinkuti, somisi
shoes nsampatu
shoot (*v.*) sika
shop makazini
shopkeeper n'tek'ya makazini
shoplifter mwîv'ya makazini
shopping basket kitunga kinsumbila
shopping center fulu kia kati kia nsumbila
shore kúmu, simu
short nkufi
shortage nsat'wa ngolo
shot sikwa, nsikwa, mbulwa; **be shot** búlwa,
shoulder vêmbo
shout bôka
show (*v.*) sônga, sôngisa / (*n.*) nsôngolo
shower mvula
shut (*v.*) kânga
sick (be sick) (*v.*) bêla
side ndâmbu
sight mbwînu
sightseeing nzietolo mu bifulu
sign sinsu
signal sinsu
signature siniatile
silver sêngwa kia mbôngo
sing yimbila
single (*n.*) bumosi, walembwa sômpa / (*adj.*)
  mulembwa sômpa
sink dimuka

sir tata
siren mâzu ma luzayisu
sister busi, mpangi ya nkênto ya se ye ngudi mosi
sit vwânda
six sâmbanu
sixteen kûmi-ye-sâmbanu
sixth n'sâmbanu
sixty makum'masambanu
size dimensio
skateboard (*n.*) tingi-tingi / (*v.*) mânta tingi-tingi
ski (*v.*) siki
skis (*n.*) zisiki
skin nkânda nitu
skirt kifunga
skull visi kia n'tu
sky zúlu
sleep lêka
sleeping bag nsâku ya ndekila, tolo
sleeping car wako dia ndêkila, tolo
sleeping pills mbuma tolo
slow malêmbe
small fiôti, n'ke
smell nsudi
smile (*n.*) kinseva-seva / (*v.*) seva kinseyila
smoke boda
smoking mboda
smooth (*adj.*) malêmbe
snack (*n.*) kiambukuta
snake nioka
snow (*n.*) neze, mvula maza ma mpembe /
  (*v.*) noka mvula maza ma mpembe
soap sabuni
soccer sombala, futubale

sock soseti
soft pete-pete
sold tekolo
sold out mana sumbwa
soldier kesa, soda
some fiûma
someone mûntu mosi
something kima, lekwa
son mwâna wa bakala
song nkûnga
soon (*adv.*) ntama-ntama
sore (*adj.*) ngânzi / (*n.*) mpasi za ngânzi
sorrow nkênda
sorry nkênda
sound mâzu
soup supu
sour nsa, n'ta
source tûku
south sudi, bânda dia nsi
soy soya
spare (*adj.*) lwenguka
spare part ndâmb'wa kiansadila
speak vova
special kiampila n'ka
speed ntînu, n'swâlu
speed limit nduta za ntînu, ndut'e nswâlu
speedometer masini mansongisila ntînu, kisonga kia ndut'e nswâlu
spell sombala
spend futila, sadila (mbôngo)
spicy yama
spider sangabudi
spine mwânz'ya nima

spokesperson nzônzi
spoon nzalu
sport nsaka
sports zinsaka
spring (*season*) kiânzu; (*water*) nto; (*metal coil*) bobini (ya nsinga sengwa)
square (*town square*) mpâmbu a mbânza; (*shape*) kale, zidi kia ndambu ya za bula bumosi
stadium sitade, bânzala kia nsaka, nzo kia, ya mbudila bâdi
staff bântu bakisalu
stairs sikalie
stamp temba
stand telama
standard busadilwânga, sitandale
start yantika, bantika
starvation n'satu
state nsya luyâlu, leta
station sitasio
statue kiteke
stay sâla
steak búdi (dia mbizi)
steal yêmba
step (*v.*) tâmbula / (*n.*) lutâmbi
sterile (*for a male*) mfwenima, (*for a female*) kisita; (*germ-free*) kikondolo mikolobe
stitch tûnga
stolen yêmbwa
stomach fûndu
stone tadi
stop telama, telamasa, nîngama
storage lûndulu
store makazini

storm mvula
stove zikwa
straight (*adj*.) sûngama / (*v*.) **go/be straight**
sûngama / (*n*.) **straight road** nzila ya sûngama
stranger nzênza
street bala-bala
strength ngolo
student nlongoki, ntawuzi, mwâna kalasi
study longuka
substitute mvingasu
suburb mbela mbanza
subway nzil'a nsya n'toto
suck fiba
suffer mona mpasi
sugar sukadi, nswikidi
suit cositime, kositime
suitcase mvwalasi
suite ndandulu, suku dia n'nene
summer mbangala
summon bôkila
sun ntângu
sunblock n'kak'wa ntângu
sunburn yokwa kwa mwînia ntângu
Sunday Kialumingu
supermarket nz'wa zându dia n'nene
supplies (*for use*) biamfunu, (*for work*) biansadila
surgeon ngânga mpasudi
surgery mpasululu, mpasudulu, mpasula
surname nkûmb'wa ngyikila
surprise nsûtuka, mbabumuka
surrender (*v*.) kivâna
suspect (*n*.) ndu bânzulu / (*v*.) bânzila
swallow (*v*.) mina

swear diá ndefi
sweat tukuta
sweet nzênzo
swelling m'vîmbu
swim tá mansaya
symbol kisînsu
symptom mbonosono
synagogue kinlôngo, tempelo
syringe ntûmbu
system sisitemi, mbwêno ya mpila nsadila

table mêza
tag labele
tail n'líla
take baka
talk mokina, yambila
tall ndâ, n'donguba
tampon bandi izieniki, nkakila ya mavunia
tape bandi manetiki
taste ntomo
tax (*v.*) futisa mpaku / (*n.*) mpaku
taxi takisi
tea ti
teacher nlôngi
telephone telefoni; **public telephone** fôni ya
  bântu babo, fôni ya bandônga; **mobile telephone**
  telefôni mobile
television televezio
tell tâ
temperature ndungutila
temple tempelo
temporary ntang'wa nkufi
ten kûmi

tenant m'futidi, mûnt'we mfutila

tent n'sâmpa kapo

territory kunkukia n'tôto

terrorist mvang'ya mambi

test tesite

thank you: I thank you ntondele, **thanks are yours** matôndo mâku, **thanks to you** matôndo kwa nge(ye)

that kina, dina, yina

theater kimpa, nz'wa kimpa (hall, room)

then (*adv.*) bôsi, lândila

there kûna, vâna, váná; **arrive there** lwâka vana; **go over there** wênda váná

they ba-/bâwu, bi-/biawu, mi-/miawu, zi-

thief mwîvi

thigh bûnda

thin siôka, fiônga

thing kima

think bânza

think for bânzila

thirst nsat'we maza

thirteen kûmi-ye-tatu

thirty makum'matatu

this didi, kiki, edi, eki, ewu, endu

thought dibânza

thousand fûnda

threat (*n.*) ndungasa

threaten dungasa

three tatu

throat ngongol'wa laka

through munzila, mu kati kwa

throw tuba, lôsa

thumb nlêmb'wa n'nêne

thunder lubandanu
Thursday Kiaya
ticket tiki
tie (*v.*) kânga / (*n.*) nkânga, kalavâti
time ntângu
tip (*n.*) vângu / (*v.*) sônga vângu
tire (*v.*) bêbisa / (*n.*) mbêbisa
today wûnu, bûnu
together kimvuka
toilet mvedoso, WC
toilet paper papie ya nkokunina
toll (*n.*) mfuta / (*v.*) futisa
tomato tumântu
tomorrow mbazi
tonight nkokila (yiyi, ya bûnu)
tool salulwa
tooth dînu
toothache (have a ~) tatikwa dînu
toothbrush bolosi kia mêno
toothpaste dentifilise
top vazulu
torture benduzula, bûba nkuba
total mbundakasa
touch nsimbulu
tourist n'ziêti
towel sume
town mbânza
trade kinkita
tradition nsalul'wa bambuta, bwasîsa bambuta
traditional ki nza nkulu, bonso bwa sîsa bambuta
traffic talafiki
trail mwâlu
train lukâlu

train station sitsio ya lukalu
transfer tambukisa, tambakasa, fila (kwa mûntu)
translate bângula
translator m'bângudi
transplant wa-nkuna, kia-nkuna, ntûnga mu
  nit'wa n'káka
transport nata
transportation ndatunu
trap (*v.*) baka, kânga / (*n.*) n'tâmbu
trash kiantuba
travel ziêta
tray palato
treat sadisa, yengisa
trespassing mviôka (va fulu kia n'siku)
trial ntêzolo
triangle zidi kia ndâmbu tatu
tribe kânda
trick (*n.*) kimpampa / (*v.*) sála kimpampa
trip nzietolo
trolley dikâlu
trouble mâmbu
truck kamio
trunk fulu kia kifunda ku nima vetile
trust (*v.*) tûdila vûvu / (*n.*) vûvu
truth ludi
try têza
true dialudi
Tuesday Kianzôle, Kiazole
tunnel nzila nsya n'toto
turn nzûnga, mbaluka
tutor nlông'ya mbaz'ya kalasi
twelve kûmi-ye-zôle
twenty makum'mole

twice nkûmbu zôle
twin bansimba
two zôle
type (*n.*) kôndo / (*v.*) búla

umbrella palapidi
uncle ngud'ya nkazi, tata mbuta
uncomfortable kiambweno mpasi
unconscious kiakondwa nzayilu
under kunsi
underground kuns'ya ntoto
understand bakisa
underwear kimpola, m'bat'ya nsi
undo bantikila, kutula
unfamiliar lembwa zayakana
unhappy lembwa, kôndwa kiese
uniform mpila mosi, inifolome
union kimvuka
United States Etazini
universe nzâ
university inivelesite, kalasi kia n'nene
unlock kangula, zibula
until ti
unusual lembwa sadilwa ntângu zazo
up (*adv.*) ku zulu
use (*v.*) sadila / (*n.*) nsadulu
usual busadilwanga ntângu zambidi
utter vova

vacancy nkondolo
vacant kóndwa
vacation mvundulu
vaccinate vâna mangwele, zênga mangwele

vaccination mvanun'wa mangwele
vanilla vaniye
vegetable ndûnda
vegetarian kidie kia ndûnda, n'die wa ndûnda
vehicle ntongobilu
veil vwale
vein mwânzi
verb mpânga
very nkati
video vidio
view mbonika
village váta
violence mvângula
virus vilusi, bivânanga bêla mu nitu
visa viza
visit (*v.*) kîngula / (*n.*) nkîngulu
visitor n'kîngudi
voice ndînga
volunteer (*n.*) munkôndwa m'futu, kisadi kia luzolo / (*v.*) sála kôndwa m'futu, sála mu nzola
vomit lúka
vote vôti, nsôlolo

wait vingila
wake sikama
walk (*v.*) tâmbula / (*n.*) ntâmbula
wall baka
wallet mpotefe
want kala ye nsatu, zola
war nkîndu
warm ndungutila
warn zayikisa, benda matu
warning m'bend'wa matu

was kedi
wash sukula
washing machine masini mansukudila nlele
watch (*v.*) tunganana / (*n.*) (*timepiece*) montele
water maza, n'kóko
we tû-
weapon vangwa kia ndwanina
wear vwâta
weather nsiens'ya kûma
wedding lôngo
Wednesday Kiatatu
week lumingu
weekday lumbu kia kisalu
weekend nsuka lumingu
weigh pêza
welcome ndwakul'we mbote
well (*interj.*) ibobo / (*n.*) (*for water*) búlu dia maza
west kudimukilanga ntângu
what bwe(yi), nki ma
wheat masa ma mputu
wheel lûlu
wheelchair kiti kia malulu
when nk'ye ntângu
where kwe(yi)
whistle (*v.*) sika, búla mpiololo / (*n.*) mpiololo
white mpêmbe
who nani
why bila (nki), diambú diá nki
wife n'kênto
wild ya mfinda
win nûnga
wind vento , mupepe
window nêla

wine malavu
wing díve
winter sivu
wipe kusuna
wire n'singa sêngwa
wireless Internet Inteleneti ya kôndwa n'singa
wisdom ndwênga
wise dia ndwênga
withdraw vola, benda, katula
withdrawal mvololo
without kôndwa
woman n'kênto
womb vumu
wood baya, lukuni
woods nkuni
wool mika mia même, lene
word m'vovo
work (*n.*) kisalu / (*v.*) sála
world nzâ
worm muntúdia
worry (*v.*) mona ntima mpasi / (*n.*) mbwêno ntima mpasi
wrap (*v.*) zînga
wrist nsîng'wa kôko
write sonika
wrong ya fwa, mbi, kabwawu ko, ka bobo ko

x-ray reyo ikis

year m'vu, mvula; **last year** m'vu uviôkele; **next year** m'vu ukwîza, m'vu ulwêki
yeast levile
yell bôka

yellow maza ma lâla
yes îh, înga, ingeta
yesterday zôno
yogurt yawulu
you nge, ngêye
young ndwêlo, n'twênia
youth kindende

zealous sakisa
zero mpavala, ka lekwa ko, ka kima ko
zipper siên'ya nkângila (kinkuti evo m'bati)
zoo fulu kiantadila bibulu biamfînda, zo

ENGLISH-KIKONGO
PHRASEBOOK

BASIC PHRASES

Hello.
Kiambote.
Mbote. / Kiambote kiaku. (*to an individual*)
Kiambote kieno. (*to more than one person*)

Hi! Mbote!
Welcome! Ndwakul'wa mbote!

Good morning.
Mbote. / Kolele. / Sikamene. / Kiambote.

Good afternoon.
Mbote. / Kolele. / Kiambote.

Good evening.
Mbote. / Kolele./ Kiambote.

Good night.
Toma leka. / Toma lambalala. / Mpimba mbote.

Do you speak English?
Kingelezo uvovanga? / Zeyi vova kingelezo?

What's your name?
Nkumb'waku nani? / Zina diaku nani?

My name is ...
Nkumb'wami ...

Pleased to meet you.
Ngyangalele mu ku mona.

How are you?
Nitu bweyi kwani? / Kolele? / Ngeye kolele?

I'm fine, thank you.
Nkolele, ntondele. / Ngyena wa mbote, ntondele.

And you?
Ye ngeye?

See you ...
Si twa monana …

soon ka ntama ko / ntama-ntama / ka zingila ko
later bilumbu bilweki / bilumbu biena kwiza /
  kunima ntamgu
tomorrow mbazi

Take care!
Toma kilunda! / Kala wa mbote!

Goodbye.
Sâla mbote. (*to someone staying*)
Wenda mbote. (*to someone leaving*)

Yes.   **No.**
Ih. / Ingeta.   Nkatu. / Ve.

Excuse me. (*to get attention*)
Ndodikila.

Excuse me. (*to pass*)
Ndemvukila. / Unsîla nlêmvo.

Okay.
Ibobo. / Kadiambu ko.

Please.
Dodokolo. / Ko.
(*Example*: **Unsadisa ko.** Please help me. /
  Help me please.)

Thank you.
Ntondele. (*I thank you.*)
Matôndo kwa nge(ye) (*Thanks to you.*)
Matôndo mâku. (*Thanks are yours.*)

You're welcome.
Ibobo. / Kadiambu ko. / Kavena diambu ko.

| **Sorry.** | **I'm sorry.** |
| Unsila nlemvo. | Mbweni kiadi. |

It doesn't matter.
Ka vena diambu ko. / Ka diambu ko.

I need ...
Nzolele … / Mvwidi mfunu …

Help!
Unsadisa!

Where is the bathroom?
Kabini veyi kyena? / WC ve kyena?

Who? Nani?	**What?** Nki?
Where? Ekweyi?	**When?** Nkia ntangu
Why? Mu diambu dia nki?	

Entrance Nkotolo
Exit Mvayikulu

open zibula
closed ye kangama
good mbote
bad mbi

this eki / edi   **here** eva
that ekio / ekina   **there** evo / evana / evanaa

Sir Tata
Madam Mama / Madami
Mr. Tata mwana bakala
Ms. Mama mwana n'kento
Mrs. Mama / Ngudia bana
Dr. (*medical*) Dokotolo /Ngânga nkisi /
    Ngânga bilôngo
Dr. (*academic*) Dokuta

LANGUAGE DIFFICULTIES

Do you speak English?
Zeyi vova kingelezo? / Kingelezo uvovanga?

Does anyone here speak English?
Vena mûntu uvovanga kingelezo?

I don't speak Kikongo.
Kivovanga Kikôngo ko.

I speak only a little Kikongo.
Kikôngo fioti kaka ivovanga.

I speak only English.
Kingelezo kaka ivovanga.

Do you understand?
Weti bakisa?

I understand.	**I don't understand.**
Ngieti bakisa.	Kieti bakisa ko.

Could you please ...?
Dodokolo lenda …?

    repeat that
    vutukila dio

    speak more slowly
    vova malimbe kibêni

    speak louder
    vova wa tumbula ndinga

point out the word for me
songa mvovo nlembo ya mona

write that down
unsosonikina dio

wait while I look it up
vingila yatala yo

What does ... mean?
... disongele nki?

How do you say ... in Kikongo?
Bwe lutelanga ... mu Kikongo?

How do you spell ...?
Bwe lusonikinanga ...?

TRAVEL & TRANSPORTATION

Arrival, Departure, and Clearing Customs

I'm here ...
Eva ngyena ...

> **on vacation** mu mvunda
> **for business** mu diambu dia kisalu
> **to visit relatives** mu tala mpangi zami
> **to study** mu kwiza longuka kalasi

I'm just passing through.
Mu mviokolo kwami ngyena. /
Vioka kwami ngyeti vioka.

I'm going to ...   **I'm staying at ...**
Ku ... ngyeti kwênda.   Ngyena kala ku ...

I'm staying for X ...
Ngyena vwanda X dia ...

> **days** bilumbu
> **weeks** tumingu
> **months** ngônda

I have nothing to declare.
Kyena ye kima kia mbôka ko.

I'd like to declare ...   **Do I have to declare this?**
Nzolele boka ...   Mfweti boka eki?

That is mine.   **That is not mine.**
Ekio kia mono.   Ekio ka kia mono ko.

```
· · · · · · · · · · · · · · · · · · · ·
·                                     ·
·            You Might Hear           ·
·                                     ·
·  Wena ye kima wa boka?              ·
·  Do you have anything to declare?   ·
·                                     ·
·  Kifunda kiki nge mosi wesedi kio?  ·
·  Did you pack this on your own?     ·
·                                     ·
·  Dodokolo zibula nsaku yiyi.        ·
·  Please open this bag.              ·
·                                     ·
·  Fweti futa mbôngo a dwani mu kiaki.·
·  You must pay duty on this.         ·
·                                     ·
·  Bilumbu kwa wena vwanda/kala kuku? ·
·  How long are you staying?          ·
·                                     ·
·  Where are you staying?             ·
·  Kweyi wena vwandila?               ·
·                                     ·
· · · · · · · · · · · · · · · · · · · ·
```

This is for personal use.   **This is a gift.**
Kiaki mono mosi isadila kio.   Kiaki kia nkabila.

I'm with a group.   **I'm on my own.**
Mu kimvuka ngyena.   Mono mosi kaka ngyena.

Here is my ...
Kiaki kia mono ...

> **boarding pass** nkânda mbantina
> **passport** pasepolo
> **ticket** tiki
> **visa** viza

You Might See

Imigrasio Immigration
Duane Customs
Ntalulu ya Pasepolo Passport Control
Mvâmbula / Mpâmbanu Quarantine
Kikongo kia besi Congo Congo citizens
Banzenza Foreigners
Kondwa futila Duane Duty-Free
Ndombolo Bifunda Baggage Claim
Nkotosolo bifunda Check-in
Pulisi Police
Ntalulu ya Sikila Security Check

Buying Tickets

Where can I buy a ... ticket?
Kwe ndenda sumbala tiki kia …?

bus bisi
plane avio / ndek
train lukalu
subway nzila ns'ya n'toto

one-way nzila mosi
round-trip kwênda-vutuka
first class nivo ya ntete
economy class nivo ya kia ntal'wa kuluka
business class nivo ya bantu babisalu

A ticket to ... please.
Dodoklo umvana tiki kimosi ku …

One ticket, please.
Dodokolo, tiki kimosi.

Two tickets, please.
Dodokolo, bitiki biole.

How much?
Ntalukwa?

Is there a discount for ...?
Nkululu kayena ko mu …?

> **children** bana
> **senior citizens** binunu
> **students** bana bakalasi
> **tourists** baturisite

I have an e-ticket.
Ngyena ye tiki kia electroniki.

Can I buy a ticket on the ...?
Ndenda sumba tiki mu ...?

> **bus** bisi
> **train** lukalu
> **boat** bato
> **subway** nzila ya nsia ntoto

Do I need to stamp the ticket?
Ya tudisa tampo va tiki?

I'd like to ... my reservation.
Nzolele ya ... leselevasio yami

change vinga
cancel vunzasa
confirm sikidika

How long is this ticket valid for?
Tiki kiki nkia ntangu kimanamfunu?

I'd like to leave ...	**I'd like to arrive ...**
Nzolele kwênda ...	Nzolele lwaka ...

today wunu kiki
tomorrow mbazi
next week lumingu lulweki/luna kwiza
in the morning mu nsuka
in the afternoon ku nima midi
in the evening mu nkokila
late at night mu mpimpa

Traveling by Airplane

When is the next flight to ...?
Ntilumu ya ndeke yi lendi nkia ntangu yena kala ...?

Is there a bus to the airport?
Bisi yena ku mu kwênda ku fulu kia ndeke?

Is there a train to the airport?
Lukalu lwena ku mu kwênda ku fulu kia ndeke?

How much is a taxi to the airport?
Ntalukwa yifutwanga mu baka takisi ku fulu kia ndeke?

You Might See

Nkotosolo Check-in
Nkotosolo ya bankwa bitiki bia E E-ticket check-in
N'kânda mbantina Boarding pass
Mbantunu Boarding
Nsikuduku Security
Ndombol'we Bifunda Baggage claim
Zansi zawonsono International
Besinsi Domestic
Zindwakulu Arrivals
Zindondokolo Departures
Bifulu bia Mvingul'wa ndeke Connections

Airport, please.
Ku fulu kia ndeke, dodokolo.

My airline is ...
Kompani dia ndek'yami i ...

My flight leaves at ...
Ntilumuka ya ndek'yami yena kala mu ...

My flight number is ...
Nomba ya ntilumuka ndek'yami yena ...

What terminal?   **What gate?**
Nkia terminale?   Nkia kielo?

You Might Hear

Nlandidi !/ Ndu lendi!
Next!

**Dodokolo twala pasepolo yaku. /
Nkand'ak'wa mbatina.**
Your passport/boarding pass, please.

Katula biabio biena mu posi kiaku.
Empty your pockets.

Katula nsampatu zaku.
Take off your shoes.

Tula biabio bia sengwa mu palato.
Place all metal items in the tray.

Nomba ya ntilumuka ...
Flight number ...

Bubu Nomba ya Ntilumuka ...
Now boarding flight number ...

Nomba ya Kielo ...
Gate number ...

Where is the check-in desk?
Bilo kia nkotosolo bifunda ekie?

My name is ...
Nkumb'wami ...

I'm going to ...
Ku ... ngieti kwênda.

Is there a connecting flight?
Ntilumuka ya mvinga ndeke yena?

I'd like ... flight.
Nzolele ntilumuka ya ...

   a direct lembwa soba ndeke
   a connecting nsobolo ndeke
   an overnight mpimpa mosi

I'd like a/an ... seat.
Nzolele kiti kia ...

   window fenetele
   aisle kati
   exit row nlonga wa kielo

Can you seat us together?
Lenda kutu vwandisa fulu kimosi?

How long is the layover?
Ntang'wa mvingila kuna fulu kia ndeke kilweki
wôla kwa yena?

Do I have to check this bag?
Yakotisa batala kifunda eki?

How much luggage is allowed?
Bifunda kwa bivanunwanga luve?

I have ...
Ngyena ye ...

 one suitcase mvalasi mosi
 two suitcases mvalasi miole
 one carry-on item kima kimosi kia ndata vakoko
 two carry-on items bima biole bia ndata vakoko

Is the flight ...?
Ntilumuka yena ...?

 on time mu wôla
 delayed kunima wôla
 canceled ya funzakaswa

Where is the baggage claim?
Kwe kwena fulu kia mbakulu kifunda?

I've lost my luggage.
Kifunda kiami kividid.

My luggage has been stolen.
Kifunda kiami kiyembolo.

My suitcase is damaged.
Mvwalis'yame wupasukidi.

Traveling by Train

Which line goes to ... Station?
Nkie nzila yikwêndanga ku Stasio ya ...?

Is it direct?
Ka yitelamanga ko mu nzila?

Is it a local train?
Lukalu lwa vava lwena?

Is it an express train?
Lukalu lwa nswâlu beni lwena?

I'd like to take the bullet/high-speed train.
Nzolele baka lukalu lwa kela/ntînu za nsisi.

Do I have to change trains?
Mfweti soba Makalu?

Can I have a schedule?
Ndenda baka ziwôla za makalu?

When is the last train back?
Lukalu lwa nsuka nkia ntangu lwena?

Which track?	**Where is track ...?**
Mu nkia nlayi?	Nlayi ... kwe wena?

Where is/are the ...?
... kwe yena/diena/kyena/miena/biena?

    dining car wako dia ndila
    information desk bilokia nsangu
    luggage lockers fulu kia nkangul'wa bifunda
    reservations desk bilo kia nsikidikila nzietolo
    ticket machine masini ma bitiki
    ticket office bilo kia bitiki
    waiting room suku dia nvingidila/ngingidila

This is my seat.	**Can I change seats?**
Kiaki kiti kiami.	Ndenda soba bikiti?

Here is my ticket.
Tiki kiami kiaki.

What station is this?
Yai nkia sitasio?

What is the next station?
Nkia sitasio yilweki?

Does this train stop at ...?
Lukalu lulu letelamanga vana ...?

Traveling by Bus and Subway

Where is the nearest bus stop?
Ntelamono ya bisi ya nkufi ve yina?

Where is the nearest subway station?
Sitasio ya nsia n'toto ya nkufi ve yena?

Which ...?
Nkia ...?

> **gate** kielo/kiavulu   **stop** ntelamasa
> **line** nkia nlonga   **station** sitasio

Can I have a bus map?
Ndenda baka kalati kia nzilaza bisi?

Can I have a subway map?
Ndenda baka kalati kia nzilaza za nsia n'toto?

How do I get to ...?
Bwe ndenda lwakila ku ...?

Which bus do I take for ...?
Nkia bisi ndenda ba ...?

Which subway do I take for ...?
Nkia nzila nsia n'toto mfweti baka mu kwênda ku...

Is this the bus to ...?
Yayi ibisi ikwêndanga ku ...?

Is this the subway to ...?
Yayi yi nzila ya nsia n'toto ku ...?

When is the ... bus to ...?
Nkia ntangu bisi ya ... yena ku ...?

> **first** ntete   **next** yena landa   **last** nsuka

How far is it?
Bula mulwaka kuna nki?

Do I have to change buses/trains?
Mfweti vinga zibisi/makalu?

Where do I transfer?
Veyi/Nkia fulu mfweti sabukila?

Can you tell me when to get off?
Lenda ku ntela nkia ntangu mfweti kulumuka?

How many stops to ...?
Ntelama zikwa ntete twa lwaka ku ...?

Where are we?
Kweyi twena?

Next stop, please!   **Stop here, please!**
Ntelama yilweki!   Telema vava! Kanga vava!

Traveling by Taxi

Taxi!   **Where can I get a taxi?**
Takisi!   Kwe ndenda bakili takisi?

Can you call a taxi?   **I'd like a taxi now.**
Lenda bokla takisi?   Nzolele baka takisi bubu.

I'd like a taxi in an hour.
Nzolele baka takisi mu wôla mosi.

Pick me up at ...   **Take me to ...**
Wiza ku mbonga vana ...   Undata ku ...

    this address adelesi yayi
    the airport banzala kia ndeke
    the train station sitasio ya lukalu
    the bus station sitasio ya bisi

Can you take a different route?
Lenda baka nzila ya n'kaka?

Can you drive faster?
Lenda tambusa nswâlu beni?

Can you drive slower?
Lenda tambusa malimbe fioti?

Stop/Wait here.
Telama/Vingila vava.

How much will it cost?
Ntalukwa ifutwanga?

You said it would cost ...
Butele ntalu yena kala ...

Keep the change.
Lunda nsiensi.

Traveling by Car

Renting a Car

Where is the car rental?
Kwe kweni vetila zamfutila?

I'd like a/an ...
Nzolele ...

> **cheap car** vetila ya ntalu ya fioti
> **compact car** vetile ya kati-kati
> **van** vane
> **SUV** VSU
> **scooter** sikutele
> **motorcycle** moto
>
> **automatic transmission** talasimisio otomatiki
> **manual transmission** talasimisio manuele
> **air conditioning** kondisionema ya mupepe
> **child seat** kiti kai mwana

I have an international driver's license.
Ngina ye permi ya nza ya mvimba.

I don't have an international driver's license.
Kien'ami ye pelemi ya nza ya mvimba.

How much does it cost ...?
Ntalukwaifwanga ...?

> **per day** mu lumbu kia mvimba
> **per week** mu lumingu lwa mvimba
> **per kilometer** mu kilometa mosi
> **per mile** mu mila mosi
> **for unlimited mileage** mu lutangu lwa mila
>   lwakondwa nsuka
> **with full insurance** asilance totale

Are there any discounts?
Zinkulula mu mbôngo zena?

What kind of fuel does it use?
Nkia kondo wa maza ma tiya yisailanga?

I don't need it until ...
Kivwid'yami yo mfunu ko te ...

> **Monday** Kiamonde / Kialendi
> **Tuesday** Kiazole / Kianzole
> **Wednesday** Kiatatu / Kiantatu
> **Thursday** Kiaya / Kianya
> **Friday** Kiatanu / Kiantanu
> **Saturday** Kiasabala / Kiansambanu
> **Sunday** Kialumingu

You Might Hear

Siya vwa garanti mfunu. I'll need a deposit.

Tula maletula mantete eva. Inital here.

Sinie eva. Sign here.

Fuel and Repairs

Where's the gas station?
Sitasio ya lesanikwe yena?

Fill it up.
Fulusa yo.

I need ... gas.
Nzolele ... lesanzi.

> **leaded** ya m'bdi
> **unleaded** yakondwa m'bodi
> **regular** ya sempele
> **super** ya supele
> **premium** ya pelemiumu
> **diesel** ya diezele

Check the ...
Tala ...

> **battery** bateli
> **brakes** zifwele
> **headlights** minda mia ntwala
> **oil** mafuta
> **radiator** ladiatele
> **tail lights** minda mia n'twala
> **tires** zipine
> **transmission** talasimisio

The car broke down.
Vetile ye fwidi.

The car won't start.
Vetile kayeti kwama ko.

I ran out of gas.
Lesanzi imbanisi.

I have a flat tire.
Pine yi mbanisi mupepe.

I need a ...
Nzolele ...

> **jumper cable** nsinga nsambukisila kwama
> **mechanic** mekaniki
> **tow truck** kamio ya mbendila

Can you fix the car?
Lenda vangulula vetile?

When will it be ready?
Nkia ntangu yena mana?

Driving Around

Can I park here?
Ndenda yo telamasa eva?

Where's the parking lot/garage?
Fulu kia ntelamasa ekieyi/garaze eyei?

How much does it cost?
Ntalukwa yifwanga?

Is parking free?
Ntelamasa ka yifutulwanga ko?

What's the speed limit?
Ntînu za ngolo veyi sisukilanga?

How much is the toll?
Mfut'wa nzila ntalukwa ikalanga?

* * * * * * * * * * * * * * *

You Might See

Telama Stop
Bika kavioka Yield
Ndambu mosi kaka One Way
Kukoti ko Do Not Enter
Nzak'wa ntînu Speed Limit

* * * * * * * * * * * * * * *

Can I turn here?
Ndenda kwami balukila eva?

Excuse me, please!
Undodikila, dodokolo!

Can you help me?
Lenda kunsadisa?

Is this the way to ...?
  Yayi nzila ku ...?

How far is it to ...?
  Nkia bula bwena mu lwaka ku ...?

Is this the right road to ...?
  Nzila yi yambote mu lwaka ku ...?

Where's ...?
Kwe kwena ...?

  ... Street Balabala ...
  this address balabala eyi
  the highway nzila ntongobilo ya n'nene
  the downtown area fulu kia vile

Where am I?
Kweyi kuku ngyena?

I'm lost.
Wa vila ngyena. / Mvididi.

Can you show me on the map?
Lenda kunsonga va kalati?

Do you have a road map?
Wena ye kalati kia nzila?

How do I get to ...?
Bweyi ndenda lwakila ku ...?

How much longer until we get to ...?
Bula bukwa busidi mu lwaka ku ...?

How long does it take ...?
Ntangu kwa yi bakanga ...?

    on foot mu malu
    by car mu vetile
    using public transportation nsalulu ya nzietolo
      mu ntongobilo ya bawonsono

There's been an accident.
Sumbula kisalamene.

Call the police.   **Call an ambulance.**
Bokila pulusi.   Bokila ambilasi

My car has been stolen.
Vetile yami yi yembolo.

My license plate number is ...
Nomba ya Palati yami yena ...

Can I have your insurance information?
Ndenda baka nsangu za asilans'yaku?

You Might Hear

Wenda kaka ku tengama ko. Go straight ahead.
Tengama ku lubakala. Turn right.
Tengama ku lumonso. Turn left.
ku ndambu yina ya balabala across the street
vana ndamb'we nsuka around the corner
ngyenda kuntwala forward
van ntwala(ya) in front (of)
mvutuka kunima backward
kunima behind
vana mpambu yilweki at the next intersection
vana mwinda talafiki wulweki at the next traffic light
landa next to
vana ntwala before   **kuna nima** after
vambêla near   **kwa nda / nsuku** far
nolo north   **sudi** south
esiti east   **wesiti** west

Baka ...
Take the ...

   kiamvu bridge
   mvayikulu exit
   nzila ntongobilu ya n'nene highway
   balabala/aveni street/avenue
   lukolongo lwa talafiki traffic circle
   mu nzil'a nsia n'toto tunnel

ACCOMMODATIONS

Where is the nearest ...?
Kwe kwena ... ya nkufi ye vava?

Can you recommend a/an ...?
Lenda ku nvana nkumb'wa ...?

> **hotel** hotele
> **inn** inni / nzo ndêka mviokila
> **bed-and-breakfast** fulu kian ndeka ye madia
>   mansuka
> **motel** motele
> **guesthouse** nzo ya banzenza
> **(youth) hostel** hositele (ya bindende)

I'm looking for ... accommodations.
Ngieti sosa fulu kia ndeka kikalanga ...

> **inexpensive** ntalu ya fioti/kiakuluka ntalu
> **luxurious** kia bankwa mbôngo
> **traditional** bonso kiasisa bambuta
> **clean** kia vedila
> **conveniently located** va fulu kiambote

Is there English-speaking staff?
Mûntu uvovanga kingelezo wena?

You Might See

Mukondolo mûntu Vacancy
Mukondolo mûntu nkatu No Vacancy

Booking a Room

I have a reservation under ...
Ye lundisi nsikidika suku mu nkumbwa ...

Do you have any rooms available?
Lwena ya suku delenda lekwa?

I'd like a room for tonight.
Mvwidi suku mfunu mu mpimpa yiyi.

I don't have a reservation.
Kie lundisi suku ko.

Can I make a reservation?
Ndenda lundisa suku?

I'd like to reserve a room ... for XX nights
Nzolele lundisa suku dia ... mu mpimpa XX.

  for one person mûntu mosi
  for two people bantu bole

  with a queen-size bed mfulu ya ntin'wa nkento
  with two beds mfulu zole

How much is it?
Ntalu kwa yeno?

How much is it per night/person?
Ntalu kwa yena mu mpimpa mosi ye mpe mu
mûntu mosi?

Is breakfast included?
Bidia bia nsuka biena mu ntalu yiyi?

ACCOMMODATIONS

Does that include sales tax (VAT)?
Mpaku (VAT) ya ntekila yena mukati kwa ntalu yiyi?

Can I pay by credit card?
Ndenda futile mu kalati kia keledi?

My credit card number is ...
Nomba ya kalati kiami eyi ...

Do you have (a/an) ...?
Lwena ye ...?

    air conditioning kondisionema ya mupepe
    business center fulu kia mâmbu ma bisalu
    cots mfulu za mwana
    crib mfulu ya mwana fioti
    elevator elevatele
    gym gimnaziumu
    hot water maza matiya
    kitchen kikuku
    laundry service masini mansukudila minlele
    linens zidala za mfulu
    microwave oven fulu kia mikolowonde
    non-smoking rooms suku dilembwa nwinwanga
      sikaleti
    phones zifoni
    pool zanga dia ntela mansaya
    private bathrooms suku dia nsukudila dia m'vwe
      kaka
    restaurant suku dia ntekila madia ye dila
    room service suku dia selevii
    safe nkela ndundila ma bai ntalu
    television televizio
    towels ziswime
    wireless Internet Interneti yikondolo nsinga

Is there a curfew?
Nsiku mia mvutuka mpimpa miena?

When is check-in?
Ntangu ya nkota nki?

May I see the room?
Ndenda tala suku dio?

Do you have anything ...?
Wena ye suku ...?

    bigger dilutidi n'nene
    cleaner dilutidi vedila
    quieter dilutidi kondwa mazu
    less expensive diena ntalu ya fioti

I'll take it.
Nzolele dio baka.

Is the room ready?
Suku diami diyilamene?

When will the room be ready?
Suku diam nkie ntangu diena yilama?

At the Hotel

room number nomba ya suku
floor ntoto
room key nsabi za suku

How can somebody call my room?
Bweeyi mûntu kalenda bokidila suku diami?

Where is the ...?
Kwe(yi) kwena ...?

bar fulu kie ndwina malavu
bathroom suku dia nsukudila
convenience store fimakazini fia nsumbila bima
dining room suku dia ndila
drugstore/pharmacy makazini ma bilongo / falamasi
elevator elevatele
information desk bilo kie nsangu
lobby fulu kia ngyambidila
pool maza ma nsukudila
restaurant suku dia nsumbila madia ye dila
shower suku dia ngyobidila

Can I have (a) ...?
Ndenda baka ...?

another room key nsabi ya n'ka ya suku
blanket vunga
clean sheets dala za vedila
pillow kuse ya n'tu
plug for the bath fulu kia kula mu suku dia ngyobidila
soap sabuni
toilet paper papela ya nkokunina
towels ziswime
wake-up call at ... mbila nsikamana mu ...

I would like to place these items in the safe.
Nzolele tula bima bibi mu nkela ndundila.

I would like to retrieve my items from the safe.
Nzolele baka bima biami mu nkela ndundila.

Can I stay an extra night?
Ndenda kudikila mpimpa mosi?

Problems at a Hotel

There's a problem with the room.
Mfwemoso mosi yena mu suku.

The ... doesn't work.

  air conditioning Condisionema ya mupepe
    kayeti sala ko.
  door lock Kumba kadieti sala kielo.
  hot water Maza matiya kamaeti sala ko.
  shower Mvula ngyobidila kayeti sala ko.
  sink (Di)longa dia nsukudila kadieti sala ko.
  toilet Wese kakieti sala ko.

The lights won't turn on.
Mwinda ka weti kwama ko.

The ... aren't clean.
... ka zena za vedila ko.

  pillows zikuse
  sheets zidala
  towels ziswime

The room has bugs/mice.
Suku binsekwa/matutu diena.

The room is too noisy.
Suku diena mazu beni.

I've lost my key. **I've locked myself out.**
Nsabi ami mvidisi yo. Yikikangididi kumbazi.

Checking Out of a Hotel

When is check-out?
Mvayikulu nkie ntangu?

When is the earliest I can check out?
Nkia wôla ya ntete ndenda vayika tekila ntangu veni?

When is the latest I can check out?
Nkia wôla ya nsuka ndenda vayika tekila ntangu yoyo?

I would like to check out.
Nzolele vayika.

I would like a receipt.
Nzolele fin'kânda fia kimbangi ki mfutidi mbôngo.

I would like an itemized bill.
Nzolele baka fakitile ya bimâmbu-mâmbu.

There's a mistake on this bill.
Foti yena mu fakitile yiyi.

Please take this off the bill.
Dodokolo katula kiâi mu fakitile.

The total is incorrect.
Mbundakasa kayena bufwêni ko.

I would like to pay ...
Nzolele futa ...

   by credit card mu kalati kia keledi
   by (traveler's) check mu sieki (ya n'zieti)
   in cash mu mbôngo

Can I leave my bags here until ...?
Ndenda sisa bifunda biami vava te ...?

Renting Accommodations

I'd like to rent (a/an) ...
Nzolele ya futilanga ...

>**apartment** apatema
>**house** nzo
>**room** suku

How much is it per week?
Ntalukwa mu lumingu?

I intend to stay for XX months
Nzolele vwanda zingônda XX.

Is it furnished?
Yena ye biamvwandila ye bia ndekila?

Does it have/include (a/an) ...?
Yena ye /mu kati mwena ye ...?

>**cooking utensils** bima bia ndambila
>**dishes** malonga
>**dryer** masinu mangyumisina
>**kitchen** kikuku
>**linens** nlele mia nzo
>**towels** ziswime
>**washing machine** masini mansukudila

Do you require a deposit?
Galanti lufutisanga mfunu?

When is the rent due?
Mbôngo za nzo nkia lumbu zifutwa?

Who is the superintendent?
Mfum'wa bisalu nani?

Who should I contact for repairs?
Nani ndenda bokila mu kubika bifwidi?

Camping and the Outdoors

Campsite Fulu kia kampema

Can I camp here?
Ndenda tula kampema yami vava?

Where should I park?
Veyi ndenda telamasa ntongobilu?

Do you have ... for rent?
Lwena ya ... ya mfutila?

> **cooking equipment** ekipema ya ndambila
> **sleeping bags** nsaku ya ndekila
> **tents** zi tanti

Do you have ...
Lwena ye ...

> **electricity** kula
> **laundry facilities** fulu kiansukudila nlele
> **showers** mvula ngyobidila

How much is it per ...?
Ntalukwa ifutwanga mu ...?

lot fulu
person mûntu mosi
night mpimpa mosi

Are there ... that I should be careful of?
Mwena ye ... bi mfweti kebila?

animals bibulu bitatikanga
insects binsekwa
plants min'ti

DINING OUT

Meals

breakfast madia man'suka
lunch madia ma midi
brunch madia ma n'suka ye midi
dinner madia ma nkokila
snack madia ma fioti-fioti
dessert madia ma nsukisinu

Types of Restaurants

bar nzo ya ndwina malavu
bistro bisitolo
buffet nzo madia mabufe
café fulu kia ndwina kafi
fast food restaurant nzo madia ma nswâlu
halal restaurant nzo ya ndila ya halala
kosher restaurant nzo ya ndila ya koshele
pizzeria nzo ya ndila piza
restaurant nzo ya nsumbila madia ye dila
snack bar nzo ya nsumbila madia mafioti-fioti
steakhouse nzo ya nsumbila ye ndila mbiz'ya ngombe
teahouse nzo ya nsumbila ye ndwina ti
vegan restaurant nzo ya ndila madia ma ndunda kaka
vegetarian restaurant nzo ya ndila madia ma
   bimenina kaka

Can you recommend a/an ...?
Lenda ku nsongidila ...?

   good restaurant nzo ya ndila ya mbote
   restaurant with local dishes nzo ya ndila madia
      ma nsi

---

inexpensive restaurant nzo ya ndia ya ntalu ya fioti

popular bar nzo ya zayakana mu nwina malavu

Reservations and Getting a Table

I have a reservation for ...
Ngyena ye ndundisa ya ...

The reservation is under ...
Ndundisa yena mu nkumb'wa ...

I'd like to reserve a table for ...
Nzolele lundisa meza ma ...

Can we sit ...?
Tulenda kweto vwanda ...?

over here eva   **over there** evana
by a window va mbela feneta
outside kumbazi
in a non-smoking area va fulu kinwinwanga fumu ko

How long is the wait?
Mvingila nkia ntangu yizingilanga?

Ordering at a Restaurant

It's for here.   **It's to go.**
Ma ndila vava.   Ma ndata mu nzila.

Waiter! Tata Kisadi!   **Waitress!** Mama Kisadi!

I'd like to order.
Nzolele tuma.

Can I have a ... please?
Dodokolo, ndenda baka ...?

   menu meni
   wine list nlonga malavu
   drink menu meni ya mandwa
   children's menu meni ya bana bandwelo

Do you have a menu in English?
Lwena ya menu mu Kingelezo?

Do you have a set/fixed price menu?
Lwena ye meni ya ntalu ya kangwa/ka yivingânga ko?

What are the specials?
Zi sipesiale inki?

Do you have ...?
Lwena ye ...?

Can you recommend some local dishes?
Lenda kunsonga madia ma vata didi?

What do you recommend?
Nki benzi ndenda sôla?

I'll have ...	**Can I have a ...?**
Nzolele baka ...	Ndenda baka ...?
What is this?	**What's in this?**
Eki nki?	Nki kitululu mu?

Is it ...?
... kyena?

> **spicy** ndungu yama
> **sweet** n'zenzo
> **bitter** ndudi
> **hot** tiya
> **cold** kiozi

Do you have any vegetarian dishes?
Lwena ye madia ma bimenina?

I'd like it with ...   **I'd like it without ...**
Nzolele kio dia ye ...   Nzolele kio dia kondwa ...

Are there any drink specials?
Sipeciale za biandwa zena?

I'll have a ...
Nzolele baka ...

> **glass of ...** kopo dia ...
> **bottle of ...** ntut'wa ...
> **pitcher of ...** mbidika ya ...

I'd like a bottle of ...
Nzolele baka ntut'wa ...

> **red wine** malavu mambwaki
> **white wine** malavu mampembe
> **rosé wine** malavu marosé
> **house wine** malavu mansala mu nzo
> **dessert wine** malavu ma madia mansuka
> **dry wine** malavu mangôla
> **champagne** sampani

A light beer, please.
Dodoklo, biele kia pepele.

A dark beer, please.
Dodokolo, biele kia ndombe.

Special Dietary Needs

I'm on a special diet.
Mu diete sipesiale ngyena.

Is this dish free of animal product?
Madia mama ka mena mbizi ya bulu ko?

I'm allergic to ...	**I can't eat ...**
Nitu ka yizôlanga ... ko.	Ki lendi dia ... ko.

  dairy bidia bia kimvumina
  eggs maki
  gelatin gelatina
  gluten guluteni
  meat nsuni
  MSG MSG
  nuts nkandi
  peanuts nguba
  seafood madia ma mbu
  spicy foods madia ma ndungu
  wheat bele

I'm diabetic.
Diabete ibêlanga.

Do you have any sugar-free products?
Lwena ya bima bikondolo sukadi?

Do you have any artificial sweeteners?
Lwena ye sukadi ya luvunu?

I'm vegan/vegetarian.
Mono ndunda/bimenina kaka idianga.

Complaints at a Restaurant

This isn't what I ordered.
Ka biabi ko ntumini.

I ordered ...
Mono ... ntumini.

This is ...
Bibi ... biena.

  cold biakiozi
  undercooked biankunzu
  overcooked biazina
  spoiled biabeba
  not fresh biankulu
  too spicy biandungu zasaka
  too tough nazukutu
  not vegetarian ka biabimenina ko

Can you take it back, please?
Dodokolo lenda bio vutukila baka?

I cannot eat this.
Kilendi bio dia ko.

How much longer until we get our food?
Nkia ntangu yisidi bosi twena baka madia meto?

We cannot wait any longer.
Kalendi diaka vingila bwanda ko.

We're leaving.
Twele kweto.

Paying at a Restaurant

Check, please!
Dodokolo, sieki!

We'd like to pay separately.
Tuzolele futa mûnt'we biandi.

Can we have separate checks?
Tulenda baka fakitile za kabwana?

We're paying together.
Twena futile vakimosi.

Is service included?
Mfut'wa kisalu wena mo kati?

What is this charge for?
Mbôngo zizi weti lomba za nki?

There is a mistake in this bill.
Foti yena mu fakitile yiyi.

Can I have a receipt, please?
Dodokolo ndenda baka n'kânda kimbangi kia mfutila?

Can I have an itemized bill, please?
Ndenda baka fakitile ya bima bia sasilwa

It was delicious!
Bia nsunga beni bikezi!

FOOD & DRINK

Cooking Methods

baked bia ndungutila
boiled bia fukuswa
braised bia makala
breaded bia yokwa
creamed bia nikwa
diced bia bukuzunwa
filleted biazenguzunwa
grilled bia ndungutila
microwaved bia fulu kia mikolowonde
poached bia kalungwa
re-heated bia yandulwa
roasted bia yangwa
sautéed bia lambwa mu mafuta
smoked bia mwisi
steamed bia mwiku
stewed bia supu
stir-fried bia lambwa kia ndikuzuna
stuffed bia kende
toasted bia babulwa

rare bia bimênga-mênga
medium rare bia kati kwa bimênga-mênga
well-done bia toma lambwa

on the side va mbela

Tastes

bitter bia ndudi	**sour** bia nsa
bland bia bututu	**spicy** bia ndungu
salty bia mungwa	**sweet** bia sukadi

Dietary Terms

decaffeinated bia katula kafina
free-range bia nima nzo
genetically modified biakudila mu nsiensi ya genetiki
gluten-free bia kondwa gulitini
kosher bia kosiele
low-fat bia mafuta makuluka
low in cholesterol bia kolesitelole ya kuluka
low in sugar bia sukadi ya kuluka
organic bia oluganiki / n'tot'wa mpamba
salt-free bia kondwa mungwa
vegan bia ndunda
vegetarian bia kimenina

Breakfast Foods

bacon mafuta ma ngulu
bread dimpa
butter manteka
cereal seleyale
cheese folomazi
eggs maki
granola galanola
honey wiki
jam kompote
jelly zeli
omelet diaki dia kalangwa
sausage bude
yogurt yawulu

Vegetables

asparagus asipalage
avocado mbuma
beans madezo
broccoli bolokoli
cabbage kabezi
carrot kaloti
cauliflower sufololo
celery seleli
chickpeas ndamba
corn sangu
cucumber kokomba
eggplant obelezine
garlic aye
lentils mbinzu
lettuce leti
mushrooms buwa
okra zenge-zenge
olives mingingie
onion niaza
peasmbwenge
pepper ndungu
potato mbumbulutela
radish ladisi
salad salata
spinach epinale
sweet potato kwa kia nzenzo
tomato lumantu

Fruits and Nuts

apricot apiliko
apple pomi
banana n'koyongo

---

blueberry mbuma za bule
cashew kasu
cherry seli
Clementine lala dia kelemantine
coconut kokoti
date dati
fig mungiengie
grape galapi
grapefruit pampelemuse
lemon lala dia nsa
lime lala dia makwanza
mandarin lala dia mandelani
melon mbuma maza
orange lala dia nzenzo
peanut nguba
peach pisi
pear pwale
pineapple nanazi
plum pulumi
pomegranate gelenate
raspberry falambwasi
strawberry felezi
tangerine lala dia tanzelina
walnut nwaseti
watermelon bundu dia maza manzenzo

Meats

beef mbizi ya ngombe
burger belegele
chicken nsusu
duck dibata
goat nkombo
ham lari
lamb meme dia n'twenia

pork ngulu
rabbit nlumba
steak siteki / budi dia mbizi
turkey nkunkuta
veal mwana ngombe

Seafood

calamari kalamali
clams palulude
crab nkala
fish mbizi ya maza
lobster munsala n'nene
mussels mbizi ya n'suni
octopus pievele
salmon somo
shrimp munsala

Desserts

cake gato
cookie sikiti
ice cream keleme ya kiozi
pastries pati
pie mukati
pudding kende
whipped cream keleme ya bufwa

Drinks

Non-Alcoholic Drinks

apple juice maza ma pomi
coffee (black) kafi (dia ndombe)
coffee with milk kafi dia midiki
hot chocolate sokola ya tiya

lemonade maza ma lala dia nsa
milk midiki
mineral water ominelale
orange juice maza ma lala
sparkling water maza ma mbabumuka
soda / soft drink soda / malavu ma n'zenzo
soymilk midiki mia soya
tea ti

Alcoholic Drinks
beer biele
   bottled beer biele kia n'tutu
   canned beer biele kia lanta
   draft beer biele kia nsi
brandy balandi
champagne sampani
cocktail kokutele
gin malvu ma zini
liqueur likele / bitatila / malavu mangolo
margarita malagalita
martini malitini
rum lumi
scotch sikoti
tequila tekila
vermouth velemautu
vodka vodika
whisky wisiki
wine vinu
   dessert wine vinu ya nsuka madia
   dry wine vinu ya yuma
   red wine vinu ya mbwaki
   rosé wine vinu ya loze
   white wine vinu ya mpêmbe

You Might See/Hear

Local Foods

Vegetables
benda kale-like leaf
bowa tall spinach-like leaf
kinsumba bitter leaf
mfumbwa forest iron leaf
ndûnda kale
nkovi kale-like leaf
nsaki kasava leaf
nsweka pumpkin-like leaf

Tubers
dioko cassava root / raw tapioca
kwa kia nguvu thick tuber
kwa kia n'zênzo sweet potato

Beans/Seeds/Nuts
madêzo beans
mbîka pumpkin-like seeds
mbwênge multicolored small beans
nguba peanut

Tropical Forest and Bush Mushrooms
bukutukutu soft ear-shaped mushroom
bunjokoto hard chewy mushroom
bunkalankala small rotten-wood mushroom
mawolumuna large portabella-type mushroom
nsempila bush mushroom
nzawu abundant bush mushroom

Pasta
kwanga boiled ground tapioca
mfundi cooked tapioca flour

You Might See/Hear

Local Foods *(cont.)*

Meats

kimboko okapi
mbala small cat-like animal
mpakasa buffalo
ngômbe beef
nkayi antelope
nkiedi squirrel
n'kuti okapi
nlumba rabbit
nsizi raccoon
ntoto black cat-like small animal
nzima civette
sima large squirrel-like animal

Edible Savannah Small Animals

fumfu pinkish rodent
kûzu big squirrel
mpuku bush rats
mfingi very small rat
mbende striped small rodent
nkáka pangolin
nkankala tiny gray rodent
sunzia white sand rat
tonga yellow rodent

Pies

kênde dia mbika pumpkin-like ground seed pie
kênde dia nguba ground peanut pie

Grocery Shopping

Where is the nearest market/supermarket?
Kwe kwena zandu dia nkufi/zandu dia supele?

Where are the baskets/carts?
Bitunga/Buluweti kwe biena?

I'd like some of this/that.
Nzolele ndambu ya ebi/ebio/ebina.

Can I have ...?
Ndenda baka ...?

    a (half) kilo of ... ndambu ya kilo ya ...
    a liter of ... litele mosi ya ...
    a piece of ... fitini fia ...
    two pieces of ... bitini biole bia ...
    a little more yikila fioti
    a little less katula fioti

Can I have a little of ... please?
Dodokolo, ndenda baka fiafioti fia ...?

Can I have a lot of ... please?
Dodokolo, ndenda baka fiafingi fia ...?

That's enough, thanks.
Fiofio fifweni, ntondele.

Where can I find ...
Kwe(yi) ndenda mwina ...?

    cleaning products bima bia nsukudila
    dairy products bima bia kimvumina

deli section fulu kia bianzengila
fresh produce bima bia ntwenia/mpa
fresh fish mbizia maza ya ntwenia/mpa
frozen foods madia makonzele
household goods bima bia nzo
meats zimbizi
poultry zinsusu / nuni za n'nene

I need to go to the ...
Nzolele kwênda ku ...

bakery fûlu kia mampa
butcher shop makazini mazengulwanga mbizi
fish market zandu dia mbizi za maza
produce market zandu za bimenina bianteka
supermarket zandu dia supele

You Might See

Teka mu dati ya ... Sell by ...
Lundila mu filigo. Keep refrigerated.
Yandula ntete wadia. Reheat before consuming.
Kosele Kosher
ologaniki organic
Biambota kwa ndie mia bimenina kaka Suitable f
for vegetarians
Lenda tula mu mikolo onde Microwaveable
Dia mu kati kwa bilumbu ... kunima nzibula
Eat within ... days of opening

Paying for Groceries

Where is the checkout?
Kesi ya mfutila veyi yena?

Do I pay here?
Ya futila eva?

Do you accept credit cards?
Lutambudilanga bikalati bia keledi?

I'll pay in cash.
Nzolele futila mu mbôngo.

I'll pay by credit card.
Nzolele futila mu kalati kia keledi.

Paper/Plastic, please.
Dodokolo, papele evo palaitika.

I don't need a bag.
Kivwidi finsaku mfunu ko.

I have my own bag.
Ngyena ya finsaku fiami.

MONEY & BANKING

Where can I exchange money?
Kwe(yi) ndenda siensila mbôngo?

Is there a currency exchange office nearby?
Bilo kia nsiensila mbôngo kyena va nkufi ye vava?

I'd like to exchange ... for ...
Nzolele siensa ... za ... mu mbôngo.

> **American dollars** dolale ya Amedika
> **pounds** siterlingi
> **Canadian dollars** dolale ya Kanada
> **euros** erosi
> **traveler's checks** sieke za nzieti
> **Congolese francs** falanka ya Congo

What is the exchange rate?
To ya nsiensi ntalukwa yena?

What is the commission charge?
Mbôngo za komision ya nsiensi ntalukwa?

Can you write that down for me?
Lenda yo kunsonikina?

Is there a bank near here?
Banki yena va nkufi ye vava?

Where is the nearest ATM?
Kweyi kwena MTA ya nkufi ye vava?

What time does the bank open/close?
Nkia ntangu banki yi zibukanga/kangamanga?

Can I cash this check here?
Ndenda bakila mbôngo za sieki yiyi vava?

I would like to get a cash advance.
Nzolele baka mbôngo za n'twala mfutulu.

I would like to cash some traveler's checks.
Nzolele baka ndambu ya mbôngo za sieki ya nzieti.

I've lost my traveler's checks.
Mvidisi sieki zami za n'zieti.

The ATM ate my card.
MTA ididi kalati kiami.

You Might See at an ATM

kotisa kalati insert card
nomba ya PIN PIN number
kotisa enter
sukula clear
anule cancel
za sieki checking
sa ndunda savings
nkatudulu withdrawal
ntululu deposit
papela ya kimbangi receipt

SHOPPING

Where's the ...?
Kwe(yi) kwena ...?

antiques store makazini ma ma bia nkulu
bakery fulu kia mampa
bookstore makazini matekwanga mabuku
camera store makazini matekwanga masini ma foto
clothing store makazini matekwanga mvwata
convenience store makazini matekwanga bima bia
   fioti-fioti
delicatessen makazini matekwanga bima bia
   delikate
department store makazini ma n'nene ma bima
   bia mpila mu mpila
electronics store makazini ma elekitoloniki
gift shop makazini ma bima bia nkaya
health food store makazini ma madia ma
   nkodidisila nitu
jeweler mûntu wa bizu
liquor store makazini ma malavu mangolo
mall fulu kia makazini makati kwa nzo
market zandu
music store makazini ma bima bia miziki
pastry shop makazini ma zipati
pharmacy makazini ma bilongo / falamasi
shoe store makazini ma nsampatu
souvenir store makazini ma bima bia mbambukila
   moyo
supermarket zandu dia supele dia kat'ya nzo
toy store makazini ma bima bia nsakanana

Where's the ...?
Kwe(yi) kwena ...?

    cashier nambudi wa mbôngo
    escalator esikalie ya bitambi
    elevator elevatele / asasele
    fitting room suku dia ntezila m'vwatu
    store map kalati kia makazini

Can you help me?
Lenda kunsadisa?

Where can I find ...?
Kwe(yi) ndenda mwina ...?

I'm looking for ...
... ngyeti sosa.

I would like ...
... nzolele.

I'm just looking.
Tala kwani kaka ngieti tala.

I want something ...
Nzolele kima kimosi kyena ...

    big n'nene / wonga
    cheap kikondolo ntalu
    local kia vata didi

    small kia ndwelo
    expensive kia ntalu beni
    nice kia mbote

I can only pay ...
Ndendele kaka futa ...

Is it authentic?
Kiaki kia ludi kiedika?

Can you show me that?
Lenda kunsonga kio?

Can I see it?
Ndenda kio mona/tala?

Do you have any others?
Wena ye kia n'kaka?

Can you ship this?
Lenda fidisa eki?

Can you wrap this?
Lenda kanga eki?

Do you have this in ...?
Lwena ye eki kia ...?

   black ndômbe
   blue bule
   brown kulele ya lukala lwa yuma
   gray kulele ya bombe
   green niâza
   orange titi kia lala
   pink mbwaki ya kiloka
   purple fumfu
   red mbwaki ya mpamba
   white mpêmbe
   yellow maza ma lala

Do you have anything lighter?
Wena ye kima kia mpembulula?

Do you have anything darker?
Wena ye kima kia nlombila?

That's not quite what I want.
Kiokio ka kiau ko nzolele.

I don't like it.
Kizolele kio ko.

I'll take it.
Ngyena kio baka.

How much?
Ntalu kwa?

That's too expensive.
Ntalu yo yiseki.

Do you have anything cheaper?
Wena ye kia kuluka ntalu?

I'll give you ...
Si yakuvana ...

I'll have to think about it.
Si ya banzila dio ntete.

Is that your best price?
Yoyo yintalu yaku yilutidi mbote?

Can you give me a discount?
Lenda kunkuludila?

Does the price include tax?
Ntalu yitudidi mpaku mu kati?

Where can I pay?
Kwe(yi) ndenda futila?

I'll pay in cash.
Mu mbôngo ngyena futila.

I'll pay by credit card.
Mu kalati ngyena futila.

Do you accept traveler's checks?
Lubakanga zisieki za nzieti?

I have a/an ...
Ngyena ye ...

> **ATM card** kalati kia MTA
> **credit card** kalati kia keledi
> **debit card** kalati kia nkatudila
> **gift card** kalati kia m'futu

SHOPPING

Can I have a receipt?
Ndenda baka n'kânda kimbangi kia mfutila

Complaining at a Store

This is broken.	**It doesn't work.**
Kiaki kia budika.	Kiaki ka kieti sala ko.

I'd like ...
Nzolele ...

> **to exchange this** ya vinga eki
> **to return this** ya vutula eki
> **a refund** mvutudila ya mbôngo
> **to speak to the manager** ya yambila ye
>   mfum'wa bisalu

_____

See also:
Grocery Shopping, page 193
At the Pharmacy, page 237

SERVICES

bank banki
barber n'tomis'ya nsuki / n'zeng'ya nsuki
dry cleaner nsukudi wa mupepe wayuma
hair salon suku dia nsuki
laundromat suku dia nsukudila minlele
nail salon suku dia ntomisina nzala
spa sona / kyoko
travel agency azanse ya n'zieti

At the Hair Salon / Barber

I'd like a ...
Nzolele ...

color kulele	**shave** katula mika
cut zengisa	**trim** kulula mika
perm peleme	

Cut about this much off.
Kulula bula bons ebu.

Can I have a shampoo?
Ndenda baka sampu?

Cut it shorter here. | **Leave it longer here.**
Zenga bwa nkufi eva. | Bika zanda eva.

At a Spa / Nail Salon

I'd like a ...
Nzolele ...

> **facial** kia zidi / kia luse
> **manicure** kia moko
> **massage** kia ndiemuzuka
> **pedicure** kia bitambi
> **wax** kia wakisi
> **aromatherapy** kia telapi ya zinsudi
> **acupuncture** ntobuzulwa n'kânda nitu
> **sauna** sona

At a Laundromat

Is there ...?
Kwena ye ...?

> **full-service** lusadisu lwa mvimba
> **self-service** kisadila
> **same-day service** lusadisu lwa lumbu kimosi

Do you have ...?
Lwena ye. ..?

> **bleach** balanko
> **change** nsiensi / mvinga
> **detergent** sabuna dia maza
> **dryer sheets** papela za ngiumisina
> **fabric softener** ndembosolo ya mvwâtu

This machine is broken.
Masini mama mafwa mena.

How does this work?
Bwe(yi) mama masadilanga?

When will my clothes be ready?
Mvwâtu miami nkia ntangu mimana?

whites mpêmbe
colors zikulele
delicates delikati

hand wash nsukudila mu moko
gentle cycle nzunga lebe-lebe
permanent press bia mfina ntangu zazo
dry clean only bia sukula kwa yuma kaka

cold water maza ma kiozi
warm water maza matiya fioti
hot water maza matiya

———————————

See also: **Banking**, page 196

NATIONALITIES & COUNTRIES

Where are you from?
Kwe(yi) wa tuka?

Where were you born?
Kwe(yi) we butulwa?

I'm from ...
Ku ...ya tuka.

I was born in ...
Ya butlulwa ku ...

Australia Australia
Canada Kanada
England Angletera
Ireland Irelande
New Zealand Newu Zelanda
Scotland Sikotilande
the United States Etats-Unis / Amedika
the United Kingdom Lwayome Uni
Wales Walezi

I'm ...
Ngyena ... / Ngina ...

American Mwesi Amedika
Australian Mwesi Australia
Canadian Mwesi Kanada
English Mwesi Angeletele
Irish Mwesi Irilande
a New Zealander Mwesi Nuvele Zelande
Scottish Mwesi Ekosi
Welsh Mwesi Welesi

FAMILY

This is ...
Endu wena ...

my husband bakala diami / n'kazi ami
my wife n'kento wami / n'kazi ami
my partner nkundi wami wa nzolwa
my mother ngudi yami
my father se diami
my older brother mbuta yami ya bakala
my younger brother nleke ami wa bakala
my older sister busi kiami kia mbuta
my younger sister busi kiami kia nleke
my cousin mpangi ami ya kanda/kise
my aunt tata diami / se diami
  paternal aunt tata ami wa n'kento / se diami
    dia nkento
  maternal aunt mama diami dia / ngudi ami
    ya nleke/mbuta
my uncle
  maternal uncle ngudi ami ya nkazi /
    ngwankazi ami
  paternal uncle tata diami / se di ami dia
    mbuta / dia nleke
my grandmother nkak'ami ya n'kênto ya
    kingudi/kise
my grandfather nkak'ami ya bakala ya kingudi/
    kise
my mother-in-law mama n'zitu ami / nzitu ami
    wa n'kento
my father-in-law tata n'zitu ami / 'zitu ami wa
    bakala
my brother-in-law nkwezi ami ya bakala
my sister-in-law nkwezi ami ya n'kênto

my step-mother ngudi ami ya n'sansi
my step-father se diami dia n'sansi
my step-sister busi kiami kia lusansu
my step-brother nkazi ami ya lusansu

RELIGION

What religion are you?
Nkia Dibundu wu sambidilanga?

I am ...
... ngyena

agnostic agonositiki...
atheist nunkondwa Nzambi...
Buddhist mûnt'wa Buda...
Catholic mûnt'wa Katolika
Christian Mukilisito
Hindu mûnt'wa Hindu
Jewish mûnt'wa Yuda / N'yuda
Muslim mûnt'wa Musilimi

INTERESTS & LEISURE

Do you like ...?
Uzolanga ...?

art arte / kingânga
cinema sindima
music miziki
sports nsaka
theater bimpa bia teatele

Yes, very much.
Yi/Ingeta, bwabwingi kibêni.

Not really.	**A little.**
Kabeni ko.	Fioti.

I like ...	**I don't like ...**
Izolanga ...	Kizolanga ko ...

Can you recommend a good ...?
Lenda songidila ... a mbote?

book buku di
CD CD (SEDE)
exhibit kizibisio / nsongosolo
museum musée
film filime
play nsakana za teatele

What's playing tonight?
Nki yena twa sakanwa nkokila yi?

What are the movie times?
Wôla za sindima nkia ntangu?

I like ... films/movies.
Filime/Sindima za/ya/kia ... izolanga.

action akisio
art arte / kingânga
comedy nsaka za teatele ya nsevisa
drama nsaka za teatele ya kiadi
foreign ya nsi za nzenza
horror nsaka za teatele ya mvangisi wonga
indie nsaka za teatele ya baindia
musical nsaka za teatele ya makinu ye yimbila
mystery nsaka za teatele ya masivi
romance nsaka za teatele ya nsevisa
suspense nsaka za teatele ya susipensi

I like ...
Yizolanga ...

baseball bazebale
basketball basiketibale
bicycling tambula mu bisikaleti
boxing zubazana nkomi
diving dimuka mu maza
football (American) futubadi ya Amedika
football (soccer) futubale dia mâlu / sombala
golf golofe
hiking manta miongo
martial arts arte malisiala
skiing lelumuka va neze
soccer futubale dia mâlu / sombala
surfing selfing mu maza ma m'bu
swimming mansaya
tennis tenisi
volleyball volebale

When's the game?
Nsaka nkia ntangu zena kala?

Would you like to go to the game with me?
Zolele kwênda ku nsaka ye mono?

What's the score?
Makôngo bwe(yi) mekina?
Makôngo kwa matululu?

Who's winning?
Nani weti nûnga?

Do you want to play?
Zolele sakana?

Can I join in?
Ndenda kwami kota?

FRIENDS & ROMANCE

What are your plans for ...?
Bwe(yi) lweti banzila mu ...?

> **tonight** nkokila
> **tomorrow** mbazi
> **the weekend** nsuka lumîngu

Would you like to get a drink?
Zolele baka kopo dia malavu?

Where would you like to go?
Kwe(yi) zolele kwênda?

Would you like to go dancing?
Zolele kwênda kina?

I'm busy.	**No, thank you.**
Kisalu kingi kyena yami.	Nkatu, ntondele.

I'd like that.	**That sounds great!**
Nzolele sala buna.	Buna bwa mbote beni!

I'm here with my ...
Ngyena vava ye ...

> **boyfriend** n'kûnd'yami wanzolwa wa bakala
> **girlfriend** n'kûnd'yami wa wanzolwa n'kênto
> **husband** bakala d'yami
> **wife** n'kênt'wami
> **partner** nkûnd'yami tuvwandanga
> **friend(s)** (ba)kûndi (b')ami

I'm ...
Mono ... ng'yena.

    single impûmpa / mono kaka
    married wasômpa
    separated wakabwana
    divorced m'fwiîl'wa longo
    seeing someone mûntu ngyena monanga

Do you like men or women?
Babakala evo bakênto uzolanga?

    I'm ...
    Mono ... ngyena.

        bisexual bisexuele
        heterosexual heteroxuele / n'zod'ya bakênto
          ye babakala
        homosexual homosekisiwele ngyena /
          n'zod'ya kumu dimosi kaka ngyena

Can I kiss you?
Ndenda kufiba munwa? / Ndenda kuvana beze?

I like you.	**I love you.**
Yi ku zolele.	Yi ku zolele.

COMMUNICATIONS

Mail

Where is the post office?
Bilo kia posita kwe(yi) kyena?

Is there a mailbox nearby?
Nkela n'kânda yena va ndambu yi?

Can I buy stamps?
Ndenda sumba timba?

I would like to send a ...
Nzolele fidisa ...

   letter n'kânda
   package/parcel paki/fipaki
   postcard kalati kia posita

Please send this via ...
Dodokolo fila eki mu nzil'a ...

   air mail ndeke
   registered mail n'kânda wa nsisa masono
   priority mail nkand wa nswâlu kibêni
   regular mail n'kânda ya mfidisa ya babo

It's going to ...
Weti kenda ku ...

   Australia Australia
   the United States Etats-Unis / Amedika
   Canada Kanada
   Ireland Irelande

New Zealand Newu Zelande
Scotland Sikotilande
the United Kingdom Lwayome Uni

How much does it cost?
Ntalukwa ufwanga?

When will it arrive?
Nkia lumbu ki kuna lwaka?

It contains ...
Mukati mwena ...

What is ...?
... nki?

> **your address** fulu kia ndwakisila nkada miaku
> **the address for the hotel** fulu kia hotele
> **the address I should have my mail sent to** fulu
>   mfweti tela bamfidisa n'kânda miami

Can you write down the address for me?
Lenda kunsonikina fulu kia min'kânda?

Is there any mail for me?
N'kânda mono wena? / Vena n'kand'ami?

International Nsi za nza ya mvimba
Domestic ma ns'yeto
postage za mfidisila mu posita
stamp temba
envelope mvolopo
postal code ya posita
customs baduani
postal insurance insuransi ya mfidisila mu posita

Telephones

Where is a pay phone?
Kwe(yi) kwena foni ya mfutila?

Can I use your phone?
Ndenda sadila foni yaku?

I would like to ...
Nzolele ...

> **make an overseas phone call** sala mbokila ya
>   nsi ya nda
> **make a local call** sala mbokolo ya nsi yiyi
> **send a fax** fila fakisi

What number do I dial for ...?
Nkia nomba ya sadila mu ...?

> **Information** Nsangu
> **an outside line** nsinga wa kumbazi
> **an operator** opelatele

What is the phone number for the ...?
Nomba ya foni ya ... nki?

> **hotel** hotele
> **office** bilo
> **restaurant** nzo ndila madia mansumba
> **embassy** ambasade

What is your ...?
... nki?

> **phone number** Nomba yaku ya foni
> **home phone number** Nomba ya foni ya nz'waku

work phone number Nomba ya foni ya fulu kiaku kia kisalu
extention number Nomba ya ekisitansio
fax number Nomba a fakisi
cell phone number Nomba ya mobili

Can you write down your number for me?
Lenda kunsonikina nomb'aku?

My number is ...
Nomba yami eyi ...

What is the country code for ...?
Kodi nki yena mu nsi ya ...

I would like to buy (a/an) ...
Nzolele sumba ...

domestic phone card kalati kia foni kia nsi yiyi
international phone card kalati kia foni kia nsi zazo
disposible cell phone kalati kia foni ya ntuba
SIM card kalati kia SIM
cell phone recharge card kalati kia foni kia ngikila mbôngo
pre-paid cell phone kalati kia foni kia kifutilwa

What is the cost per minute?
Ntalukwa mu minuti mosi?

I need a phone with XX minutes.
Kalati kia minute XX nzolele.

How do I make calls?
Bwe(yi) ndenda tudila zimbokolo?

collect call mbil'a mfutila kwa ndu bokolo
toll-free mbil'a nsinga ya ngovo
phonebook buku dia foni
voicemail n'kânda mvovo

On the Phone

Hello? Alo?
This is ... ... ndundu.

May I speak to ...?
Ndênda vova ye ...?

... isn't here. May I take a message?
... kena va ko. Ndenda ku m'bakila n'samu?

I would like to leave a message for ...
Nzolele sisa n'samu kwa ...

Sorry, wrong number.
Dodokolo, nomba ya mbi beki.

Please call back later.
Dodokolo, bokila ntang'wa n'kaka.

I'll call back later.
Si yabokila ntang'wa n'kaka.

Goodbye.
Sâla mbote. / Wenda mbote

Computers and the Internet

Where is the nearest ...?
Kwe(yi) kwena ... ya nkufi ye vava?

Internet café Inteleneti Kafe
computer repair shop nzo ya nsadisila odinatele

Do you have ...?
Wena ye ...?

available computers ziodinatele zeti lembwa
sadilwa
(wireless) Internet Inteleneti (ya kondwa nsinga)
a printer masini ma imprimé
a scanner masini ma sikane

How do you ...?
Bwe(yi) wu ...?

turn on this computer zibudilanga odinatele
log in kotilanga mo
connect to the wi-fi kangamananga mu wi-fi
type in English budila mu Kingelzo

How much does it cost for ...?
Ntalukwa ifwanga mu ...?

15 minutes minuti kumi ye tanu
30 minutes minuti makum'matatu
one hour wôla mosi

What is the password?
Mvovo wa nkotisila nki?

My computer ...
Odinatel'yami ...

> **doesn't work** ka yeti sala ko
> **is frozen** masono ka meti nikka ko
> **won't turn on** ka yeti kwama ko
> **crashed** yi bulangene/budizikidi
> **doesn't have an Internet connection** ka yena ye
>   nkangama ye Inteneti ko

Windows Zifeneta
Macintosh Makintosi
Linux Linuxi

computer olidinatele
laptop laputopu
USB port polote USB
ethernet cable kabele ya inteneti
CD CD (SeDe)
DVD DVD (DeVeDe)
e-mail e-mail (emele)

PROFESSIONS

What do you do?
Nki(e salu) wusalanga?

I'm a/an ...
... ngyena.

accountant Kontabele / N'tang'ya mbôngo
admisistrative assistant Nsadis'ya n'yadi
aid worker Nsadis'ya kisadi
architect Akitekite
artist Atisite / Ngangula
assistant N'sadis'ya mbela
banker Kisadi kia banki
businessman Mfum'wa bakala ya bisalu
businesswoman Mfum'wa n'kento ya bisalu
carpenter Salapantie
CEO Mfum'wa n'nen'ya bisalu (PDG)
clerk Kalaka
consultant Konsilita / N'sông'ya mâmbu
construction worker N'tung'ya nzo
contractor Kisadi kia kontala
coordinator Unwizasi
dentist Ngânga meno
director N'twadisi/dilekitele
doctor Ngânga bilongo / Dokotolo
editor Editele / N'tangudidi
electrician Kisadi kia kula / Elekitilisie
engineer Enzeniele
intern Sitaziele
journalist Zulunalisite / Nsonik'ya nsangu
lawyer Avoka / Zulisite
librarian Bibiliotekele
manager Manazele

nurse Mfwelemi
politician Politisie
secretary Sekeletele
student Mwana kalasi kia n'nene
supervisor N'tadi bisalu
teacher N'longi
writer N'soniki

I work in ...
... isadilanga

academia Akademi
accounting Kontabilite / Ntangul'wa mbôngo
advertising Mbwangasa nsangu za ntekolo
the arts Ziarte / Bingânga
banking Nsaduku ya banki
business Bizinesi / Bisalu
education Ndongolo za bantu
engineering Kinzeniele
finance Mambôngo
government Luyalu
journalism Kiansonoko za nsangu
law Kia minsiku
manufacturing Kian'sal'wa bima
marketing Kia n'tek'wa bima
the medical field Kian'kodosol'wa nitu za bantu
politics Kiapolitiki
public relations Kianzayasana ye bantu
publishing Kiambwangasana nsângu za sonukwa
a restaurant Nz'wa nsumbila madia ye dila
a store Makazini
social services Bisalu biamvwandulu za bantu
the travel industry Bisalu bia nzietolo

BUSINESS INTERACTIONS

I have a meeting/appointment with ...
Ngyena ye lukutakanu/mbwabwana ye ...

Where's the ...?
Kwe(yi) kwena ...?

> **business center** kati dia bizinisi
> **convention hall** nzw'a n'nene ya ngwizani
> **meeting room** suku dia lukutakanu

Can I have your business card?
Ndenda baka kalati kiaku kia bizinisis?

Here's my name card.
Kalati kyena nkumbwami kiaki.

I'm here for a ...
Ngyena vava mu diambu dia ...

> **conference** lukutakanu
> **meeting** mbwabwani
> **seminar** seminele

My name is ...
Nkum'wami ...

May I introduce my colleague ...
Ndenda kusonga n'kund'yam'ya kisalu ...

Pleased to meet you.
Ngyangalele mu bwabwana yaku.

I'm sorry I'm late.
Mbweni kiadi vo ndandidi.

You Might Hear

Ntondele bu wizidi/lwizidi.
Thank you for coming.

Vingila fioti, dodokolo.
One moment, please.

Ntang'wa lukutakanu yena yâku?   Ye nani?
Do you have an appointment?   With whom?

W-/K-...
He/She ...

   wena mu lukutakanu / mu lukutakanu kena
   is in a meeting

   ena mu nzietolo za bizinisi
   is on a business trip

   wena mu mvunda / mu mvunda kena
   is away on vacation

   vayikidi bubu kiki / bubu kiki kavayikidi
   just stepped out

   ndweki kantama ko / ngyena kwiza
   will be right with you

   wena kutambula bubu
   will see you now

Dodokolo vwanda va kiti.
Please have a seat.

You can reach me at ...
Lenda ku mbaka vana ...

I'm here until ...
Ngyena kala vava tee ...

I need to ...
Ngyena ye nsat'wa ...

> **make a photocopy** sala fotokopi
> **make a telephone call** bokila mu telefoni
> **send a fax** fidisa fakisi
> **send a package (overnight)** fidisa fipaki (mpimpa mosi)
> **use the Internet** sadila Inteneti

It was a pleasure meeting you.
Kiese kikezi yame mu bwabwana yaku.

I look forward to meeting with you again.
Ngyena ye vuvu vo si ya bwabwana diaka ye ngeye.

Business Vocabulary

advertisement ntelol'wa min'sumbi
advertising salu kia ntelol'wa min'sumbi
bonus n'sumbi
boss mfum'wa kisalu
briefcase maleti / fimvwalisi
business bisalu / bizinesi
business card kalati kia bisalu / kalati kia bizinesi
business casual (dress) mvwâtu (wa veva) wa kisalu
business plan pula ya bisalu/bizinesi
casual (dress) mvwâtu waveva
cell phone number nomba ya foni mobile

certification ndongolo za kimbangi kia nzayil'wa kisalu

certified nkwa kimbangi kia nzayil'wa kisalu

colleague nkund'ya kisalu

company kompani

competition ndwanunu

competitor kinwani kia ndambu ya n'kaka

computer odinatele

conference lukutakanu

contract kontala

course nzioka / ndongolo

cubicle ficazie

CV nsangu za luzingu / CV (seve)

deduction nkulululu / nkatudulu

degree dekele

desk mêza ma kisalu/bilo

e-mail address adelesi ya n'kânda wa elekitoloniki

employee kisadi / nsadi / mûnt'wa kisalu

employer mfum'wa kisalu / nkwa kisalu

equal opportunity mbonokono ya mpila mosi

expenses zindilu za mbôngo / zinvayikusulu za mbôngo

experience nzayilu ya mankulu

fax number nomba ya fakisi

field fulu kia zibuka

formal (dress) mvwâtu wa kisalu

full-time kisalu kia wôla zazo

global kia nza ya mvimba

income mbakul'wa mbôngo

income tax mpak'wa mbakul'wa mbôngo

insurance ensilase

job kisalu

joint venture bisalu biantwadi

license lisansi / luve

mailing mfidusul'wa n'kânda
marketing nsanguza ntekolo
meeting lukutakanu
minimum wage mbôngo za m'fut'wa kisalu zifweti
  futwa
multinational kompani dia sinsi zambidi
office bilo
office phone number nomba ya foni ya bilo
paperwork min'kânda mia nsina
part-time ndamb'wa ntang'wa kisalu
printer masini ma tinta kia masono
profession kisalu kia mbutisila mbôngo
professional kia kisalu kia mbutisila mbôngo
project kisalu kyena salwa
promotion ntombokolo ya mfun'wa kisalu/kisadi
raise ntombudila mbôngo za m'futu
reimbursement mvutudul'wa mbôngo
resume bunkufi
salary mbôngo za mfut'wa kisalu
scanner masinu ma sikane
seminar seminele
suit kositime
supervisor mfum'wa bisalu
tax ID ID ya mpaku
tie kalavanti
trade fair fwale kia nteki mia bia mumbôngo
uniform mvwat'wa mpila mosi/inifolome
union kimvuka
visa viza
wages mbôngo za m'fut'wa kisalu
work number nomba ya kisalu
work permit luve lwa kisalu

MEDICAL

At the Doctor's Office

Making an Appointment

Can you recommend a good doctor?
Lenda kumfila kwa dokotolo dia mbote?

I'd like to make an appiontment for ...
Nzolele sala ntangu mbwabwani mu ...

   today lumbu kia wunu / bûnu kiki
   tomorrow mbazi
   next week lumingu lulweki / lumingu lukwiza
   as soon as possible ntama-ntama

Can the doctor come here?
Dokotolo lenda kwiza vava?

What are the office hours?
Wôla za kisalu mu bilo nki?

It's urgent.
Dia nswâlu kibêni. / Dia nzaki.

I need a doctor who speaks English.
Nzolele dokotolo divovanga kingelezo.

How long is the wait?
Mvingila nkia bula yena?

```
· · · · · · · · · · · · · · ·
·              You Might Hear              ·
·                                          ·
·  Wena ye mfwemoso za alelezi?            ·
·  Do you have any allergies?             ·
·                                          ·
·  Bilongo wena nwanga?                   ·
·  Are you on any medications?            ·
·                                          ·
·  Sina eva.                              ·
·  Sign here.                             ·
· · · · · · · · · · · · · · ·
```

Ailments

I have ...	I need medication for ...
... -ena yami.	Bilongo mvwidi mfunu kadi ...

allergies Alelzi z
an allergic reaction Leakisioya alelezi y-
arthritis Nsong'wa mianzi w-
asthma Nsong'wa mfulumuna w-
a backache Nsong'wa nima w-
bug bites Tatikwa kwa binsekwa k-
chest pain Nsong'wa ntulu w-
a cold Nsong'wa kiozi k-
cramps Nkangama min'suni
diabetes Diabeti
diarrhea Salwa / Lutwa vumu
an earache Tatikwa kutu
a fever Nitu tiya
the flu Mazunu
a fracture Tolukwa visi
a heart condition Bêla kwa n'tima
high blood pressure Tansio ya saka tombuka
an infection Enfekisio / Mpasi za

indigestion Tatikwa vumu / Bêla mbûmba
low blood pressure Tansio ya saka kuluka
pain Mpasi
a rash Makwânza
swelling M'vîmbu
a sprain Mfusuka
a stomachache Tatikwa vumu
sunburn Yokwa kwa ntangu
sunstroke Zubwa kwa mwîni
a toothache Lunzwa dînu
a urinary tract infection Mpasi za nzila ya masuba
a venereal disease Bêla kwa miânzi mia mbutisilu

I'm ...
... ngina.

anemic Munkondwa mênga
bleeding Mvayikwa mênga
constipated Nkângama vumu
dizzy N'zungan'ya meso
having trouble breathing Mu fulumuna mpasi
late for my period Mu nzingila ya mvayika mênga
  ma ngônda
nauseous mu nsat'wa luka
pregnant mu vumu kia mbutila
vomiting ndukulu

I've been sick for ... days.
Bilumbu ... ya belele.

It hurts here.
Mpasi ngieti mona eva.

It's gotten worse/better.
Mpasi zitomene saka. / Zitomene kuluka.

You Might Hear

Fulumuna bwa nda. Breathe deeply.
Dodokolo kofula. Cough please.
Dodokolo, katula m'vwâtu. Undress, please.
Mpasi yeti sa? Does it hurt here?
Zibula nw'aku. Open your mouth.

budika broken   **toluka** broken   **fisuka** sprained
tambakana contagious   **sambakana bêla** infected

Fweti kwênda tala balutidi ngangu.
You should see a specialist.

Fweti kwênda ku lupitalu.
You must go to the hospital.

Nza vutuka mu tumingu tole.
Come back in two weeks.

Wena ye mfun'wa landulwa.
You need a follow-up.

Ngieti kusonikina ...
I'm prescribing you ...

   ziantibiotiki antibiotics
   ziantivirale anti-virals
   mazi mankusa an ointment
   n'katudi mia mpasi painkillers

... fweti sala.
You need ...

   Tesite ya mênga a blood test
   Ntumbu an injection
   Nzila kati kwa mwanzi (IV) an IV
   Ekizame kia mpasi za laka a strep test
   Sitelepitokoki a strep test
   Ekizame kia masuba a urine test

Treatments and Instructions

Do I need a prescription medicine?
Sono kia bilongo mvwidi mfunu?

Can you prescribe a generic drug?
Lenda kunsonikina bilongo bia babo?

Is this over the counter?
Biena kwani va meza ma falamasi?

How much do I take?
Bikwa mfweti sadila?

How often do I take this?
Bwe(yi) nkumbu kwa mfweti bio sadila?

Are there side effects?
Mpasi za mbêla bikalanga?

Is this safe for children?
Ka biambi ko kwa bana?

I'm allergic to ...
Alelezi zikalanga yami mu ...

> **antibiotics** ziantibiotiki
> **anti-inflammatories** antienfalamansio
> **aspirin** asipilini
> **codeine** kodeine
> **penicillin** penisilina

Payment and Insurance

I have insurance.   **Do you accept ...?**
Asilanse yina yami.   ... lubakanga?

How much does it cost?
Ntalukwa ifwanga?

Can I have an itemized receipt for my insurance please?
Ndenda Baka fakitile ya bimâmbu-mâmbu mu kuma kia asilansi yami?

Can I pay by credit card?
Ndenda kwami futile mu kalati kia keledi?

Will my insurance cover this?
Asilansi yame si yafutila eki?

At the Optometrist

I need an eye exam.
Nzolela sadisa kizami kia meso.

I've lost ...
Mvidisi ...

> **a lens** lupe ya disu diami
> **my contacts** zikontaki zami zameso
> **my glasses** nguya zami

Should I continue to wear these?
Mfweti landila vwata zizi?

Can I select new frames?
Ndenda sola montile zampa?

How long will it take?
Bula bwa ntangu kwa zina baka?

I'm nearsighted.	**I'm farsighted.**
Kimonanga bwankufi ko.	Kimonanga bwanda ko.

At the Dentist

This tooth hurts.
Dînu edi tatika dieti tatika.

I have a toothache.
Dînu ngieti tatikwa.

I have a cavity.
Bulu diena yami mu dînu.

I've lost a filling.
Mfulusa mosi mvidisi.

My tooth is broken.
Dînu diami dibudikidi.

Can you fix these dentures?
Lenda sala meno ma mvingasa mama?

My teeth are sensitive.
Meno mami zwezumuka mena.

You Might Hear

Vwidi mfun'wa mfulusa.
You need a filling.

Ntumbu ngyena kuvana.
I'm giving you an injection.

Anesitezia ngyena kuvana.
I'm giving you a local anesthetic.

Mfweti katula dînu didi.
I have to extract this tooth.

Kudie kima ko te ku nima wôla ...
Don't eat anything for ... hours.

At the Gynecologist

I have cramps.
Minsuni mieti ku ndikuka/nkangama.

My period is late.
Mênga mami ma bukento malandila mena.

I have an infection.
Enfekisio yena yami.

I'm on the Pill.
Mu pilile ngyena.

I'm not pregnant.
Kyena ye vumu ko.

I'm ... months pregnant.
Vumu kia ngônda ... kyena yami.

My last period was ...
Mênga mami ma bukento mansuka makala ...

I need ...
Nzolele ...

> **a contraceptive** nkangul'wa mabuta
> **the morning-after pill** pilile ya mbazi-nsuka
> **a pregnancy test** kizami kia nkadul'wa vumu
> **an STD test** kizami kia maladi venerienne

At the Pharmacy

Where's the nearest (24-hour) pharmacy?
Kwe kwena falamasi (ya wôla 24) nkufi ye eva?

What time does the pharmacy open/close?
Nkia ntangu falamasi ikangamanga/izibukanga?

Can you fill this prescription?
Lenda kumfulusila olodinase eyi?

How long is the wait?
Bula bwa mvingila bwe yena?

I'll come back for it.
Si ngiza vutuka mu baka bio.

What do you recommend for (a/an) ...?
Nki lenda songidila mu diambu dia ...?

   allergies alelezi
   cold kiozi
   cough ntul'wa nkofula
   diarrhea nduta vumu
   hangover mpasi za nkolwa
   motion sickness mpasi nzungana mu zulu evo
      va n'toto
   post-nasal drip mazunu ma maza ku laka
   sore throat mpasi za laka
   upset stomach tatikwa vumu

Do I need a prescription?
Mfweti baka olidinase?

You Might See

Sadila ...
Take ...

   kunima madia after eating
   ntete waleka before bed
   ntete wadia before meals
   mu nsuka in the morning
   mu vumu kia mpamba on an empty stomach
   mu n'nwa orally
   nkumbu zole mu lumbu twice daily
   wa nwina bio mu maza mayingi with plenty
      of water

va mbaz'ya n'kanda nitu kaka
for external use only

mina bia m'vimba
swallow whole

bilenda vâna nkolwa
may cause drowsiness

kusangasa ye alikolo ko
do not mix with alcohol

I'm looking for ...　　**Do you have ...?**
... ngyeti sosa.　　Wena ye ...

aftershave bilongo bia kunima zenga nzevo
anti-diarrheal bilongo bia nkangila vumu
antiseptic rinse bilongo bia n'nwa bia antisepitiki
aspirin asipirini
baby wipes papela zankusunina mwana
bandages bitendi bia mputa
cold medicine bilongo bia mazunu
conditioner (hair) kondisionele (dia nsuki)
condoms zipelezevatifi / zikapoti
cotton balls bimbadi-mbadi bia mavunia
dental floss nsinga mpwasika za meno
deodorant kikatula nsudi ya nitu
diapers zikuse
gauze tendi kia vunia
hand lotion mafuta mamoko
ibuprofen ibupolofeni
insect repellant bilongo bia nkumina bintudi moya
moisturizer mafuta ma maza mu n'kanda nitu
mouthwash bilongo bia nsukudila n'nwa
razor blades mbele za lazwale
rubbing alcohol alukolo ya nkusa mu nitu
shampoo sampu
shaving cream keleme ya nzevo
soap sabuni
sunblock n'kak'wa mwini
tampons zitampo
a thermometer telemometele
throat lozenges bombo za laka
tissues zimuswalu
toilet paper papela ya hiziene
a toothbrush bolosi kia meno
toothpaste sabuni ya meno
vitamins zivitamini

PARTS OF THE BODY

abdomen banda vumu
anus nwa funi
appendix nsuka ndia n'nene
arm ntand'wa koko
back nima
belly button n'nkumba
bladder subulu
bone visi
buttocks mataku
breast beni
chest ntulu
ear kutu
elbow kinkoso
eye disu
face zidi / luse
finger nlembo
foot tambi
gland nkandi
hair nsuki
hand koko
heart n'tima
hip bunda
intestines ndia
jaw tama
joint yikamu
kidney mfiangu
knee kinkoso
knuckles binkofi
leg kulu
lip koba

liver nsoko
lung fulukutu
mouth n'wa
muscle n'suni
neck nsingu
nose mbombo
penis mvia
rectum funi
rib lubanzi
shoulder vembo
skin n'kânda nitu
stomach fundu
testicles makata
thigh bunda
throat ngongol'wa laka
thumb nlemb'wa n'nene
toe nlemb'wa n'nene wa kulu
tooth / teeth dînu / meno
tongue ludimi
tonsils mbuma za laka
urethra mwanz'ya masuba
uterus fulu kia mwana mu vumu
vagina nzini
vein mwanzi wa mênga
waist luketo
wrist nsing'wa koko

GENERAL EMERGENCIES

Help!	**Fire!**	**Thief!**	**Police!**
Lusadisu!	Tiya!	Mwivi!	Pulusi!

Quickly!   **Be careful!**
Nswâlu! / Sa nzaki! / Mu ntînu!   Keba!

It's an emergency!   **I'm lost.**
Diambu dia nswâlu!   Mvididi.

There's been an attack!
Mûntu zubulu!

There's been an accident!
Sumbulu kikedi koko!

Call ...!
Bokila ...!

> **an ambulance** ambilasi
> **a doctor** dokotolo
> **the fire department** depatema ya n'zimi mia tiya
> **the police** polisi

You Might See

Mantînu / Manswâlu / Manzaki Emergency
Lupitalu Hospital
Pulusi Police
Bilo kia Pulisi Police Station

Is anyone here ...?
Mûntu wena mumu ...?

    a doctor dokotolo
    trained in CPR watwadiswa / walongwa mu CPR

Where is the ...?
... kwe yena?

    American embassy Ambasada ya Amedika
    bathroom Suku dia ngyobidila
    hospital Lupitalu
    police station Bilo kia polisi

Can you help me?	**Can I use your phone?**
Lenda ku nsadisa?	Ndenda sadila fon'yaku?

Stop!	**Stop it!**
Telama! / Kanga!	Yambula sala bobo!

Go away!	**Leave me alone!**
Katuka! / Wenda Kwaku!	Ungyambula!

Talking to Police

Please show me your badge.
Dodokolo unsonga makalo yaku.

I've been ...
Bantu ba ...

    assaulted nzubidi
    mugged nzionene bima
    raped ntele / zumba kiakingolo
    robbed ngibidi
    swindled nkosele

That person tried to ... me.
Mûntu ndunanga tezele ... mono.

    assault zuba
    mug ziona ma bia
    rape zumba kia kingolo ye
    rob yiba

I've lost my ...   **My ... was stolen.**
Mvidisi ... (ki)ami.   ... ki(bi)yembolo

    bag(s) ki(bi)funda
    credit card kalati kia keledi
    driver's license pelemi ya ndatina ntongobilo
    identification n'kânda nzayilu ya mûntu
    keys nsabi
    laptop lapitopi
    money mbôngo
    passport pasepolo
    purse fisakosi
    traveler's checks sieki za nzietila
    visa viza
    wallet mpolotofe

Please take me to your superior.
Dodokolo undata kwa mfum'waku.

Please take me to the police station.
Dodokolo undata ku sitasio ya pulusi.

I have insurance.
Ngyena ye kuveletile ya asulansi.

I need a police report.
Ngyena ye nsat'wa lapol'wa polisi.

Kwe(yi) kwa kadila diambu didi?
Where did this happen?

Nkia ntangu diambu didi diasalama?
What time did it occur?

Bweyi kena sungamanwa?
What does he/she look like?

This person won't leave me alone.
Mûntu ndu kazolele yambula kuntokanasa/
kunkwamisa/kumfwemisa ko.

My son/daughter is missing.
Mwan'ami wabakala/wan'kento vididi.

He/She is XX years old.
Mwana wena mvula ... za luzingu.

I last saw the culprit XX minutes/hours ago.
Nkumbu ya nsuka mbweningi kinati kia mâmbu
kiki XX wole iviokele.

What is the problem?
Nkia diambu?

What am I accused of?
Nkia diambu ngieti fundulwa?

I didn't realize that it wasn't allowed.
Kitekele zaya ko vo kyena ye luve lwa sala dio ko.

You Might Hear

mfwasakanu ya luvuvamu disturbing the peace

mfwasakanu za ndatunu ya n'tongobilu traffic violation

mbongo za nsik'wa ntelamasu n'tongobilu parking fine

tiki kia mviokosol'wa ntînu speeding ticket

mviokosol'wa ntangu ya viza yaku overstaying your visa

bwivi theft

I apologize.
Ndombele nlêmvo.

I didn't do anything. | **I'm innocent.**
Kivengi diambu ko. | Kyena mvang'ya mambi ko.

I need to make a phone call.
Nzolele bokila mûntu mu foni.

I want to contact my embassy/consulate.
Nzolele zayisa ambasade/kosulati yami.

I want to speak to a lawyer.
Nzolele ya vova kwa nzonz'ya n'siku.

I speak English.
Kingelezo ivovanga.

I need an interpreter.
Nsekod'ya mâmbu mvwidi mfunu.

NUMBERS

Cardinal Numbers

1 one mosi
2 two zôle
3 three tatu
4 four yá
5 five tânu
6 six sâmbanu
7 seven nsambwadi
8 eight nâna
9 nine vwa
10 ten kûmi
11 eleven kûmi-ye-mosi
12 twelve kûmi-ye-zôle
13 thirteen kûmi-ye-tatu
14 fourteen kûmi-ye-ya
15 fifteen kûmi-ye-tanu
16 sixteen kûmi-ye-sâmbanu
17 seventeen kûmi-ye-nsambwadi
18 eighteen kûmi-ye-nâna
19 nineteen kûmi-ye-vwa
20 twenty makum'mole
21 twenty-one makum'mole ye mosi
22 twenty-two makum'mole ye zole
30 thirty makum'matatu
31 thirty-one makum'matatu ye mosi
32 thirty-two makum'matatu ye zole
40 forty makum'maya
50 fifty makum'matanu
60 sixty makum'masambanu
70 seventy lusambwadi
80 eighty lunâna
90 ninety luvwa

100 **one hundred** nkama
101 **one hundred and one** nkama ye mosi
200 **two hundred** nkama zole
500 **five hundred** nkama tanu
1,000 **one thousand** funda
10,000 **ten thousand** mafunda kumi
100,000 **one hundred thousand** mafunda nkama
1,000,000 **one million** kiazi

Fractions

one-quarter ndambu mosi ya biya
one-half ndambu mosi ya kati
three-quarters ndambu tatu za ziya
one-third ndambu mosi ya zitatu
two-thirds ndambu zole za zitatu

all zawo(nsono)
none ka yimosi ko

Ordinal Numbers

first ntete
second n'zole
third n'tatu
fourth n'ya
fifth n'tanu
sixth n'sambanu
seventh nsambwadi
eighth n'nana
ninth m'mvwa
tenth n'kumi

QUANTITIES & SIZES

one dozen ma kumi ye zole
half a dozen ndambu ya kumi ye zole
a pair of ... zizole za ... / bibiole bia ...
a couple of ... biole bia ...
some (of) ... fiuma fia ...
a half ndambu
a little fioti
a lot yambidi / ya yingi
more bidi   **less** yafioti
enough yifweni   **not enough** ka yifweni ko
too many maviokele / bilutidi mbidi
too much masakidi

extra small (XS) ndwelo kibêni (TP)
small (S) ndwelo (P)
medium (M) kati-kati (M)
large (L) n'nene (G)
extra-large (XL) n'nene beni (TG)

big n'nene
bigger luta bunene
biggest toma luta bunene

small fioti
smaller luta fioti
smallest toma luta fioti

fat ya mafuta   **skinny** fionga

wide wonga   **narrow** sioka / fionga

tall n'donguba   **short** nkufi   **long** nda

WEIGHTS & MEASUREMENTS

inch zi-insi
foot tambi
mile mila
millimeter milimeta
centimeter santimeta
meter metele
kilometer kilometele

squared kale
cubed kibe

milliliter mililitele
liter litele
kilogram kilogalami

ounce awunsi
cup kopo
pint pinta
quart kwalate
gallon galon

TIMES & DATES

Telling Time and Duration

What time is it?
Nkia ntangu tweka?

It's 5 A.M./P.M.
Wôla ya 5 (n'tanu)

A.M / P.M.
Nt.M (Ntwala Midi) / Nm.M (Nima Midi)

It's 6 o'clock
Wôla ya 6 (n'sâmbanu) tweka.

It's 6:30.
Wôla ya 6:30 (n'sâmbanu ye ndambu) tweka.

five past three
minuti tanu kunima tatu

half past two
wôla ya n'zole ya ndambu

quarter to eight
minuti kumi ye tanu va ntwala wôla ya n'nana

twenty to four
minuti makum'mole va ntwala wôla ya n'ya

noon midi
midnight n'ding'wa nsi

In the ...
Mu ...

    morning n'suka
    afternoon ku nima midi
    evening nkokila

at night mu mpimpa
early n'twala ntangu
late nima ntangu

at 1 P.M.
Mu 1 Nm.M (Mu wôla ya ntete ku nima midi)

at 3:28
Mu 3:28 wôla ya n'tatu ye minuti makum'mole ye nana

for ...
mu ...

one month ngônda mosi	**two months** ngônda zôle
one week lumingu lumosi	**three weeks** tumingu tatu
one day lumbu kimosi	**four days** bilumbu ya
one hour wole mosi	**half hour** ndamb'wa wôla
one minute minuti mosi	**five minutes** minuti tanu
one second seknde mosi	**five seconds** sekonde tanu

since tuka / katuka   **during** mûntangu yi

before mûntete   **after** kunima

one year ago
mvu/mvula mosi wu/yi viokele

five years ago
mvu/mvula tanu mi/zi viokele

six months ago
ngônda sambanu zi viokele

in two years mu mvu miole
in five months mu ngônda tanu
in two weeks mu tumingu tôle
in twelve days mu bilumbu kumi ye zole
in three hours mu wôla tatu
in five minutes mu minuti tanu
in ten seconds mu sekonde kumi

yesterday zono
today wunu
tomorrow mbazi

week lumingu
month ngônda
year mvu / mvula

this week lu lumingu
next week lumingu lukwiza
last week lumingu luviokele/lukezi

this month yi ngônda / ngônda yiyi
next month ngônda yi lweki / yena kwiza
last month ngônda yi viokele/kezi

this year mvu wuwu / wu mvu yiyi / wu mvula
  yiyi / yi mvula
next year mvu/mvula yena kwiza
last year mvu/mvula wu/yi viokele / wu/yi kezi

Days of the Week

Monday Kiamonde
Tuesday Kian'zole
Wednesday Kian'tatu
Thursday Kian'ya
Friday Kian'tanu
Saturday Kiasabala
Sunday Kialumingu

Months of the Year

January Zavie / Ngônda ya ntete
February Fevilie / Ngônda ya nzole
March Malasi / Ngônda ya n'tatu
April Avili / Ngônda ya n'ya
May Mayi/ Ngônda ya n'tanu
June Yuni / Ngônda ya n'sambanu
July Yuli / Ngônda ya nsambwadi
August Agusita / Ngônda ya n'nana
September Sepitemba / Ngônda ya m'vwa
October Okutoba / Ngônda ya n'kumi
November Novemba / Ngônda ya kumi ye mosi
December Desemba / Ngônda ya kumi ye zole

Seasons

Winter Sivu / Nsûngy'a kiôzi
Spring Kiânzu / Nûng'ya n'sasu minti
Summer Mbangala / Nsûng'ya mini mia ngolo
Fall/Autumn Nsotuka makaya / Ngyuma makaya
  / Otoni